"The Dark God—Exploring the Male Shadow is possibly the most necessary book for women at this time. Especially for feminists, mothers, daughters, sisters and lovers of men, this is our most important work—to bring into a healing balance both sides of our soul. We are in this together and Marcia Starck has provided a soul-making experience for both genders with her word medicine. Thank you Ms. Starck for being a change agent for our sustainable evolution. Recommended for men too."

—Jeannine Parvati Baker, author of *Hygeia: A Women's Herbal, Pre-natal Yoga and Natural Birth,* and co-author of *Conscious Conception: Elemental Journey Through the Labyrinth of Sexuality.*

"The Dark God is an exciting invitation—with mythic backgrounds, suggested rituals, and psychological insights—to encounter that male you most miss, your unknown potential locked away in your shadow. I welcome back our sensuality, grief, humor, anger, sexuality and earthiness that Marcia Starck helps men find in these lunar gods of our richly darkened depths."

—Glenn A. Mazis, author of *The Trickster, Magician, and Grieving Man: Reconnecting Men with Earth.*

"At a time when energies of both men and women are needed to balance our world, *The Dark God* is a courageous step in that direction. As a man and a member of the Earth Community, I want to send Marcia Starck faith and support for the success of her book."

—Robert Boissiere, author of *Po Pai Mo—The Search for White Buffalo Woman, The Hopi Way, Meditations with the Hopi, Return of the Pahana,* and *Homo Spiritus.*

"Marcia Starck shows how we can use ancient Myth and modern Magic to come to terms with the male shadow. In so doing, we learn how to heal both ourselves and the land."

—Alan Richardson, author of *Earth God Rising, Twentieth Century Magic,* and *Priestess—The Life and Magic of Dion Fortune.*

Other books by Marcia Starck:

WOMEN'S MEDICINE WAYS
Cross Cultural Rites of Passage

THE DARK GODDESS
Dancing with the Shadow

THE COMPLETE HANDBOOK OF
NATURAL HEALING

EARTH MOTHER ASTROLOGY

ASTROLOGY
Key to Holistic Health

The Dark God—
Exploring the Male Shadow

by Marcia Starck

with illustrations by Rohmana Harris
and personal experiences by Rick Ramirez and
Barton Stone

ISBN 0–9644232–0–0
Library of Congress Catalog Card Number: 95–90171

First printing, March 1995
Printed in the United States of America

To contact the author, write:
Earth Medicine Books
PO Box 5435, Santa Fe, NM 87502

EARTH MEDICINE BOOKS

PO Box 5435 ⊕ Santa Fe, NM 87502
505-473-1464

Dedicaton—

To Grandmother Moon,
resplendent in the dark night,
who helps us to see our shadows.

for Richard Rittenberg, Lestor Cantor, Phil Rosen,
and in memory of Mason Kassel

Biographical Information—

ROHMANA D'AREZZO HARRIS, a California artist from the Bay area, has been an exhibiting painter for many years. Her work in this book creates images that reflect archetypes of ancient/future themes. Her development as an artist has been with art as Integral Healing. She currently teaches art as healing and therapy.

BARTON STONE, MA. is a free–lance minister using his many talents to celebrate the revival of Goddess spirituality and Nature worship while serving the community through teaching, personal counseling and ceremonial circles. A sculptor, he fashions figures on Nature and Goddess themes in stone and clay. Barton is co-director of the Great Round, a non-profit organization exploring ways of restoring personal connection to the Earth, and also the founder of the Men's Pledge of Responsibility, an organization of pro-feminist men pledged to work with male violence.

RICK RAMIREZ, MSW, is a clinical social worker helping troubled adolescents and families in the central mountains of northern New Mexico. He is developing a cross–cultural model for adult and adolescent "Rites of Passage" through a synthesis of ancient initiation practices and modern research in anthropology, mythology and psychology. Rick lives in Santa Fe and is a student of Eastern spirituality.

Table of Contents—

Acknowledgments—

With gratitude and thanks to the following people who were instrumental in birthing this book:

Rohmana Harris for her insightful art work on the cover and in the drawings of the gods; Alma and Gordon King for their skill and artistry in designing the lay out of the book; Barton Stone and Rick Ramirez for sharing and writing up their personal experiences; Sally Euclare for her careful editing and her humor.

John Stoltenberg, Robert Lawlor, Alan Richardson and Glenn Mazis for their books that inspired me and fed my vision; Dr. Howard Teich for his work on the Lunar and Solar male; Robert Boissiere, Tom Pinkson, Rick Ramirez and Jeremiah Weser for insights shared in conversations.

Brigid Fuller at Crossing Press for her help; Kathleen Potter and Sarah Harwell from the Ark Bookstore; Mary Morell of Full Circle Books and Gail Vivino for their support and suggestions; my women's circles in Santa Fe and California for their feed-back and wisdom.

FOREWORD—

he Dark God—*Exploring the Male Shadow* is a book about working with the male shadow, that unconscious repressed part of the male psyche. It is a companion volume to *The Dark Goddess—Dancing with the Shadow* which was published by The Crossing Press in 1993. Though the Jungian term "shadow" is used, this book does not represent Jungian thinking.

Various myths of male gods are used in this book to illustrate the particular part of the shadow in discussion. Not all these gods are "dark gods" in the sense that they represent the underworld or death and transformation in the way the Dark Goddess does. There were few "dark gods" because the gods were generally thought to be solar or light beings, whereas goddesses were ruled by the moon. I use the term "dark god" metaphorically to speak of those parts of the male psyche still in darkness, in the deep unconscious. Gods like Dionysus and the Horned god **are** more lunar than solar because they derive from cultures which celebrated and revered the earth, along with the feminine spirit.

The concept of "dark" or "black" is not a negative one. Darkness is as important to our survival as light; black and white are the yin and yang of our existence. In Japan, white is the color of mourning rather than black; this implies a different way of perceiving physical death. Mastery in the martial arts is acknowledged by a black belt, equating black with the highest level of skill.

For many men, the male psyche represents virgin territory. Too busy achieving in the outer world to explore their inner depths, they are often unconscious of their motivations and their own psychological backgrounds. This is true as well for some women, though women, in general, have done more exploration into this unchartered region.

We live in a time when our male cultural heroes are falling from grace. Witness the case of O.J. Simpson, a football super-star and Hollywood celebrity who violently abused his wife. Only by the brutal stabbing of her and her male friend (which appears to have been done by OJ himself) was his private life brought into public awareness. What if he had delved into his own psyche and become aware of his own insecurities? What if he had seen that he needed **power over** others because he lacked **power within?** He could not then have continued to play the myth of Mars, the all powerful and mighty god, who related to others through violence and passion.

To replace these old cultural heroes with new ones is to perpetuate the hierarchy implied by the term hero. In their stead, we have new models and prototypes for men which are based on re-connecting them to their feminine part and to their earth–based heritage. Such books as John Stoltenberg's *Refusing to be a Man* (1989) and *The End of Manhood* (1993), Robert Lawlor's *Earth Honoring—The New Male Sexuality* (1989) and the more recent book by Glenn Mazis—*The Trickster, Magician, and Grieving Man* (1994), explore these new themes and dimensions.

Regardless of our gender, we each have a lunar and solar part of our being which is often termed feminine and masculine or yin and yang. As a woman, it is as necessary for me to connect with my solar part as with my lunar. Having written a book on the Dark Goddess and the female shadow, my next assignment was to explore the other half, the male shadow. This exploration has led me to uncover parts of my own male side and to speak to many men about their male shadows. Two of these men share their experiences in the chapters dealing with the myths of the gods. Both were brought up in the dominant culture and were strongly influenced by patriarchal teachings. Each had to find his place as a lunar male by exploring his own depths and by rejecting both Christianity and the "war monger" mentality prevalent in the fifties and sixties.

This book is written for women as well as men; as women, we need to understand the deep recesses of the male psyche and explore our own inner male. When women and men can sit in circles and share their own shadows, we can begin to heal the wounds between the sexes that have persisted for centuries. Only when we can explore and understand the unconscious will it be possible to work together consciously, in the light of day, as sisters and brothers and as children of the Earth Mother.

Marcia Starck

July 1994
Santa Fe, New Mexico

Chapter 1

INTRODUCTION

Yin and Yang are the Oriental terms for the polarities of the Universe; these are sometimes translated as feminine and masculine, dark and light, receptive and active. Within the feminine and masculine there is also a dark and light side. The light side is our conscious being that we show to the world; the dark side is often referred to as the "shadow" and consists of our unconscious.

The "shadow" (a term coined by Carl Jung which is now in common usage) usually refers to a segment of one's own being which has split off and remains in the unconscious. It is a part of the personality that lies close to consciousness and may actually become a splinter personality. In addition to the personal shadow, there is also the collective shadow. The collective shadow belongs to the collective unconscious and refers to elements that society has cast in the shadow. For example, white European society has placed people of color in the shadow as well as women, especially their sexuality. The Virgin Mary has been celebrated for her saintliness while Mary Magdalene has been denigrated for being a "whore". Eve has been blamed for humanity's woes because she ate the apple and befriended the serpent, a symbol of wisdom from the older Goddess worshipping cultures. "Black" people are still considered inferior and less intelligent than "white" people and only now in 1994 are they being given the voting privilege in South Africa.

Jung stated that the ego and the shadow are formed simultaneously and are necessary to one another just as dark is necessary to light.

Our shadow may be a frightening part of ourselves, but it is not necessarily a negative part. We tend to repress those elements that are the most alive because we fear that they will be criticized by our parents, teachers, spouses, or society in general. The shadow often contains more primitive and child-like qualities that we have been afraid to show to the world. When we access those qualities and bring them into consciousness, we become more alive, exciting, and interesting.

The shadow is often projected as the experience of the "other guy", the twin, brother, or best friend who becomes the scapegoat for the qualities we don't want to acknowledge in our own beings. The Germans call this the *doppelganger*, the double or mirror image. By placing all the qualities that we feel to be negative or evil on another person, or in the case of the collective unconscious, on another country, race, or ethnic minority, this person or group becomes the scapegoat for our feelings, and we become justified in persecuting the individual or group. As an example, let's look at the relation between George Bush and Saddam Hussein. Bush tried to extricate himself from all his deceptions, illegal maneuverings and dishonesty in general by projecting all his negativity onto Hussein. Playing the "good guy", he enhanced his popular appeal and presented himself as a "deliverer" from evil forces. In a psychological sense, this enabled Bush to feel clean because he did not have to acknowledge these traits in himself.

The traits that we project onto others may not just be negative or evil. We may also project high and worthy traits onto a person and tend to "hero worship" her or him. We may project strength, power, compassion onto another because of our own fear of seeing these in ourselves. As a society, we do this through movies and television and certainly in our novels. We create characters who are beautiful and loving, or conversely, malevolent and cruel, and then tend to identify with these characters. The popularity of the film *Gone with the Wind* shows how many women have identified with Scarlet O'Hara and men with Rhett Butler.

When we react intensely to the sensuality, anger, greed, inactivity or laziness of someone else, we should look into ourselves; this very same quality may be a part of our shadow. In *A Little Book on the Human Shadow* Robert Bly refers to our shadow as the bag we carry behind us. He gives the example of a man putting his wildness, sexuality and aggression into the bag and then opening it up thirty years later and feeling both frightened by it and hostile to those feelings, which now have a more primitive quality, having been repressed for so many years.

Many ancient cultures cleansed themselves of the shadow side through the ritual sacrifice of one person or a group of people. In his book, *Owning Your Own Shadow*, Robert Johnson tells us about the origin of the "bogey man" in India. Each community chose a man to to be killed at the end of the year and take the evil deeds of the community with him. Until his death he was not required to work and could have anything he wanted. This bogeyman was deemed powerful and feared since he represented the collective shadow.[1]

Other cultures engaged in elaborate ceremonies known as the "Mysteries" to get in touch with the underworld and all that it represents—death, darkness, fears and anxieties. In this way, the dark side became a reality and was integrated with the light side. The practice of the Mysteries culminated in Greece with the Eleusinian Mysteries, which had both Greater and Lesser rites.

The greater Eleusinian Mysteries spanned nine days during which initiates went through diverse processes and purifications to prepare them for the final event, which has often been described as previewing one's death.

In Christianity, however, the dark and light sides became polarized and were termed "good" and "evil" or "God" and "Satan". Our society still acts under this dichotomy when it brands earth–based religions as "evil" and homosexuality as the work of the "Devil". This terminology, along with the structure of churches, especially the Catholic church, which use an intermediary to reach the God-head, has placed enormous fear in people and robbed them of their individual power and spiritual ability.

THE MALE SHADOW

The male shadow came into the spotlight in the feminist movement of the 60's and the resurrection of the ancient religion of the Goddess by Marija Gimbutas and others. The male shadow is very different from the female shadow. (See *The Dark Goddess— Dancing With the Shadow* for a discussion of the female shadow).

"The dark side of men is clear. Their mad exploitation of earth resources, devaluation and humiliation of women, and obsession with tribal warfare are undeniable," writes Robert Bly in his preface to *Iron John*.[2] What Bly and others in the Men's Movement have suggested is that certain ancient myths have ignored the deep feelings of men and assigned man "a place in the sky, instead of the earth."[3] These ancient myths referred to are post-patriarchal myths rather than the earlier myths where the male god is seen as the Horned One, the Green Man, the Shivaite ecstatic. So whereas the dark side of man may be power hungry and greedy, needing to rape countries as well as women, this is not necessarily all the "shadow" entails. If the male shadow were truly being expressed, if man could let go to his deep wildness and sensuality, his emotional caring and nurturing aspects, he might not need to rape, war on others, or assert his dominion over the earth. It is because these parts of man were so repressed by patriarchal religions—Christianity, Judaism and Islam in particular, that his natural urges have been totally perverted.

How many men have held back their tears when they were upset, killed others in battle when it hurt their souls, and polluted the earth because they worked for a company whose motive was greed and profit?

How many have refused to go to war, have quit their jobs for big corporations, have protected women and children in times of danger?

Unfortunately, there have been many more who have done the former than the latter because the prevalent attitude in our culture is that men must be strong, Mars-like in their behavior, "macho", aggressive. Men are not supposed to be Venusian—soft, emotional, creative and compassionate. How many men have been called "wimps" or "faggots" when they have shed tears or displayed sensitive feelings? How many have been burned at the stake or crucified? It has always been easier to carry the sword than to raise the chalice.

In the Western world, hundreds of years of patriarchy have brought the repression of emotions, sensitivity, and sexuality as well as the abusive treatment of women and the earth. Historically, the seed for this began in the Age of Aries, when conquerors and hunters from Northern Europe invaded the agricultural matriarchal cultures of the South. Before this time, in the Age of Taurus, earth-based spirituality was at its peak and the Goddess/God flourished.[4]

We have less information on when this shift occurred in Africa and in the Orient. Only recently has society learned of the tortures of women through genital mutilation in Africa, or footbinding in China and the practice of **suttee** in India. Thanks to the work of Mary Daly (see her book *Gyn Ecology* and Alice Walker's recent novel *Possessing the Secret of Joy*) we are aware of women being tortured in many parts of the world, much of which continues to happen today.

If we look at the cosmic perspective, we see that earth creatures are situated between the planet Mars and the planet Venus. Venus is on our warm side, the side that goes toward the Sun. Mars is on our cold side, the side that moves away from the Sun. If it is truly our path to individuation to move toward the light, i.e. to bring things out into the open, then all of us earth beings, regardless of gender, need to develop Venusian traits of lovingness, compassion, and creativity. This does not imply that we should ignore Mars. Aggression, confrontation of situations, and manifestation of our will and energy are totally necessary, but need to be tempered by Venus. This is the principle behind the myths of Venus and Adonis, Cybele and Attis, Isis and Osiris. It is the hierogamos or sacred marriage, the female principle working alongside the male.

MYTHS OF THE GODS

The myths of many of the Gods reveal qualities that are associated with the male shadow. Studying these myths, as well as performing ritual, can enable men to understand and connect with their own shadows and empower them. It is also important for women to understand the shadow side of men, so they can support and help in the birthing process of this unconscious area.

Many of the myths included in this book are about pre-patriarchal Gods. Shiva, Pan, Cernunnos, and Dionysus are Lunar Gods rather than Solar Gods, Earth Gods rather than Sky Gods. Each of them suffered, often at the hands of others. Many of them have made sacrifices. Many of them have "feminine" traits.

Other myths are here too—myths of post-patriarchal Gods like Hades/Pluto and Ares/Mars—who destroyed, raped and went to war. Between these two sets of myths lies some important truth. When one is not able to express his Dionysian nature, it may end up as Mars or Pluto.

RITUAL

Ritual is related to myth in the sense that both deal with symbolic acts. In myth there is a story told utilizing certain characters and events; in ritual, the symbols include objects placed on the altar, words used in invoking the directions and acts that are performed symbolically in order for certain events to occur on the material plane. For example, planting of blue corn seeds at a Spring Equinox ritual is symbolic of the new energy we are seeding at this time of year.

Through the use of ritual and ceremony, many parts of the shadow may be expressed, brought into consciousness, and then integrated into the personality. The rituals and ceremonies suggested in this book incorporate ancient and modern traditions borrowed from cultures all over the world. None involves sacrifice, bloodletting, fasting or sexual abstinence as ways of pacifying the Dark Gods or demonic forces, or their own shadows. To the contrary, these rituals expand the self, allowing greater joy, passion and wildness.

Using drums, rattles, dance, mime, chants, prayers, affirmations and other techniques in safe, secluded settings, thousands of men have visualized, tried on and integrated those parts of their personalities that they once stuffed into their bags. All emerged as healthier, vital human beings.

ENDNOTES

[1] Johnson, Robert, *Owning Your Own Shadow*, p.33.

[2] Bly, Robert, *Iron John*, Preface, x.

[3] Ibid.

[4] see the work of Marija Gimbutas—*The Language of the Goddess, The Civilization of the Goddess.*

Invocation to DIONYSUS

Oh Dionysus,

Twice born one,

Dancing in ecstasy

with your women initiates.

Rescuing Ariadne

when she was abandoned

by Theseus.

Hunting with the wild

creatures,

Sharing with us

the sacred juice

from your vine.

Dionysus
an adaptation from the well-known floor mosaic at Pella

Chapter 2

WILDNESS AND ECSTASY—
THE MYTH OF DIONYSUS

hy are men not supposed to show their primitive child-like qualities of ecstasy, joy in experiencing their bodies and the earth, playfulness in being one with the animals and the birds? When did men change from wearing loose, colorful robes and togas to dull, formal suits with ties around their necks (holding back their throat chakras)?

Wildness, ecstasy, and sensuality are intrinsic male qualities but ones most men are afraid to show to the world. Instead, men tend to be calm, rational, and un-feeling. Behind this mask lie their passions and aggressions; it is often only with a woman they trust or a woman they don't know at all (a prostitute or someone they might pick up in a bar) that they allow these strong emotions to speak. Many women have related stories to me of their husbands' never shedding a tear except once or twice when they were alone in bed. Sometimes it's easier for men to exhibit their feelings with a stranger who has never known them. They then become passionate, exciting creatures, living out much of their repressed selves.

The history of religion, as well as certain myths of the Gods, provides us with some clues. From very early times, there have been two types of religions—those that were connected to the earth and her cycles, and those that were based around urban life and human laws claiming divine origin. These laws served to make **man** central and **his** ambitions foremost. The rest of the natural order, animal and vegetable species, and **women** became subservient. The invasions of the Nomadic hordes in Europe beginning in the fifth century B.C.E. were a prime catalyst in the annihilation of earth–based religions. These nomadic tribes plundered and destroyed many of the elements of earth–based spiritual practices as the goddess and god figures. In fact, the ancient Hebrews, a group of nomadic tribes, introduced the belief in monotheism, one God, and made all other goddesses and gods idols of "pagan" worship.

In Western culture, Christianity took the process one step furthur as did Islam. Now ONE MAN became God, or his servant, and all humanity, men and women alike, modeled themselves on that one man. The institution of a church became empowered to judge each person's actions and set standards of "morality" or "immorality". Any behavior that seemed "natural," animal–like or wild, was not acceptable. All earth–based religious practices, worship of Goddesses and Gods, any display of caring nurturing qualities as well as wild sensual qualities went underground, where they have remained.

Wildness and ecstasy did not entirely disappear however. Shivaite sects in the East, Dionysian sects in the West and practicing pagans throughout Europe kept these qualities alive. The Christian church did its best, in the Inquisition, to burn, bury, and destroy earth-based religions which included all nurturing and healing modalities. The Church fathers projected their own repressed sensuality on women and accused them of fornicating with the Devil (who was half animal). They still were not successful in stamping out Nature and natural cycles. Pantheistic beliefs and cults surfaced throughout history and reminded humanity that gods and goddesses are present in all things. However, urban and industrial societies never allowed mystical or ecological points of view to enter mainstream thought. The great wisdom of the Sufis, the Kabbalists, and the ancient Essenes were continually pushed aside and labeled "esoteric".

MYTH OF DIONYSUS

Dionysus was the illegitimate child of Zeus and Semele. Zeus visited Semele at her father's palace where Dionysus was conceived. Hera, always jealous of Zeus' affairs, disguised herself as Semele's nurse and suggested to Semele that she ask Zeus to prove his immortal origins by showing himself to her in his Olympian splendor. Semele begged Zeus to do so, and was subsequently consumed by the flames of the thunderbolt that emanated from him. The child in her womb also would have perished but for a thick piece of ivy which wound around the columns of the palace and made a screen between the unborn baby and the celestial fire. Zeus took the infant, not yet ready to be born, and enclosed it in his thigh. When the time was right for its birth, he summoned the aid of Ilythia.[1] And so Dionysus had a double birth.

Zeus gave his son to Ino, Semele's sister, and her husband Athamas. But Hera's jealousy, still aching for vengeance, struck Ino and Athamas with madness and they tried to murder him. For the second time, Zeus rescued his son, changed him into a goat and had Hermes deliver him to the nymphs of Nysa.[2]

Dionysus wandered the mountains and forests with the nymphs, and early on became connected with the natural forces. As an adult, Dionysus discovered the fruit from the grape vines and learned how to make wine. He may have drunk too much of the wine at first (or Hera may have inflicted him with madness). Whatever the case, Dionysus went to Dodona to consult the oracle and healed himself.[3]

Dionysus' travels and adventures took him all over the Greek world and to Asia Minor. Typically he was accompanied by his tutor Silenus and many of the Satyrs and Maenads carrying ivy twined staffs tipped with pine cones, swords, serpents, and bull-roarers.[4] In Phrygia the fertility goddess Cybele initiated him into her mysteries and it was there that the orgiastic rites became part of his cult as it spread throughout Egypt, Syria, Lebanon, Libya, and India. When he returned to Greece, Dionysus had changed from a rustic god to a god-like man who was effeminate and soft, wearing long robes.[5]

During his travels he met Ariadne, who had been abandoned on the island of Naxos by Theseus. Dionysus made Ariadne his wife and they had three sons together.[6] He also descended into Hades where he found his mother Semele, and brought her back to life. They ascended Mt.Olympus, he re-named her Thyone (raging queen) and she became an immortal.[7]

WORSHIP OF DIONYSUS

The worshipers of Dionysus were primarily Greek women. In his celebration, referred to as "Orgia," intoxicating wine was used as well as music from drums, cymbals, and reed pipes to help the participants reach an ecstatic state where they felt possessed by the God.

In certain cases the climax of the "Orgia" was the tearing to pieces and eating of the raw flesh of a sacrificial animal, which was thought to be an incarnation of Dionysus. In Boeotia, Chios, and Lesbos, human sacrifice was actually practiced.[8]

Many festivals celebrated Dionysus; the most well known were the Greater Dionysia at the beginning of March where dramatic plays were presented. The smaller orgiastic rituals took place on the slopes of Mount Cithaeron.[9] Orgiastic cults in Asia Minor and Palestine celebrated the Canaanite Feast of Tabernacles which was originally a Bacchanalian orgy. In Thrace and Phrygia beer orgies were celebrated.[10] Wine was first imported in jars from Crete.

Dionysus was first depicted as a bearded man with an ivy crown but later became an effeminate beardless youth, wearing either an animal skin or a long robe. His head was crowned with vine leaves and bunches of grapes and he carried the pine cone in his hand.[11]

Hera's hatred of Dionysus and his wine cult reflects conservative opposition to the ritual use of wine and the wild Maenad fashion which had spread from Thrace to Athens, Corinth, Sicyon, Delphi, and other cities. Eventually, in the late seventh and early sixth centuries B.C.E., the tyrants of Sicyon, Corinth and Athens decided to approve the cult and founded official Dionysian feasts. At this time Dionysus and his vine were acccepted on Mount Olympus and Hestia was ousted from her position to make room for Dionysus.[12]

The worship of Dionysus also had a strong place in Orphism (a theological movement in the sixth century B.C.E. named after the mythical poet, Orpheus.) In Orphic theology, the infant Dionysus was torn to pieces and devoured by two jealous Titans, but his heart was saved by Athena and he was re-born through Zeus, in some versions as the son of Semele. He was worshiped as Zagreus, the Orphic name of the underworld Dionysus.[13]

The Orphics emphasized Dionysus' role as the one who conquers death. Later Orphic accounts held that Dionysus was the son of Persephone, the Queen of the dead. Thus Dionysus' cycle of death and re-birth followed that of Persephone, who spent half of her time above ground with her mother Demeter. Here the connection with the Orpheus myth is obvious—Orpheus descended and returned from the underworld to rescue his beloved Eurydice. The Orphics' main intent was to create a salvation religion in which Dionysus' triumph over death was connected to their hope for an after–life.[14]

Like the Dionysians, the Orphics connected sexuality and religion. They looked forward to a happy after–life that included sexual practices from this life.[15]

INTERPRETATION OF DIONYSUS MYTH

Dionysus, unlike other Gods, had a double birth. His mother died at his first birth; he was born from the thigh of his father at his second birth. Dionysus was brought up primarily by women, the nymphs on Mount Nysa.

In the various myths surrounding Dionysus, he is depicted as helpful to women. He rescued Ariadne who was left on an island by Theseus and later married her. He also went to the underworld to seek out his mother Semele and brought her to Mount Olympus.

In many respects, Dionysus has a more feminine quality than a masculine one. His acts are motivated by altruistic feelings not by hopes of a reward or praise for his bravery or courage as in the case of Hercules, Theseus, and other Greek heroes. He does not rape or assault women; instead he helps and supports them.

Dionysus was also highly criticized—for being a wanderer (no stability), for using an intoxicant to enter a higher state, for the acts he created when he was "mad" (though in the myth, his bouts of "madness" were caused by Hera).

There are many archetypes present in the Dionysus myth—the one who dies and is re-born as a child, the eternally youthful one, the one who goes underground and is transformed. Another archetype is that of the man seeking the ideal feminine, the mother-wife-lover.

RELEVANCE OF DIONYSUS TO MODERN MEN

WILDNESS

How have men lost the qualities of wildness, ecstasy, sensuality, nurturing? What changes individually and collectively are needed to bring them back?

Dionysus constantly went out into nature, never knowing what he would find. He traveled to different countries as well and developed a strong empathy with the spirits of the animals and plants. He was a Shaman who had an ecstatic vision of the world.

In primitive societies, men were responsible for food and shelter. They went out into nature, hunted animals and often returned to their villages with wounds, frostbite, over exposure to sun and wind. Life was a constant dance with the wilderness and the unknown forces. This challenge led them to develop spiritual practices in which they took on the beings of various animals. Sometimes they actually wore the skins of the animals (today in Taos Pueblo both deer skins and buffalo skins are worn for the dances that honor these animals); sometimes only a part of the animal was used, as for example, deer antlers. They imitated their movements and learned to communicate with them telepathically.

As Robert Bly says, "Men dared to enter the realm of animals, engage them, fight them, wrestle with the soul of the animal, learned their dances, crossed through the veil to them. Some men, called shamans, entered into the realm of the spirits as well, wrestled with them, outwitted them, and saved people who had become ill through the mischievous activities of those spirits."[16]

The more we as a society have controlled the wilderness, the more we long for it. Not only do we crave this uncontrolled wildness in nature, but in our own psyches as well.

Many men play golf or tennis when they're not inside their over-heated offices; others take up skiing, back packing, mountain climbing, and hunting, to connect with nature and draw on their inner and outer strength to complete their self-designated tasks. In Native American culture, adolescent boys are taken on Vision Quests to prepare them for sustaining themselves in nature and to strengthen them spiritually by enabling them to feel at one with the animals, plants, birds, waters, earth, sun, moon, and stars.

One of our strongest archetypes in America is the cowboy. The cowboy and the "wild West" antidote the logical rational mindset of most men in this country. Many indulge their shadow by watching Westerns on television and at the movies. By watching the killing of Indians they sublimate their own desires to strangle their bosses and supervisors.

Another strong male archetype is the "outlaw". The outlaw is the rebel who doesn't work the nine to five job, doesn't support his wife and kids, doesn't cut the grass on the week-ends. The outlaw follows his own **individual** path. At his best, he wants to break traditions; he cares about others and helps them as well. Robin Hood, our most popular outlaw, is joined in modern times by Gandhi, Martin Luther King, and Malcolm X. "The outlaw," writes Sam Keene, "is a supranormal individual who cares about others too much to accept the limitations on eros that are imposed by normal life. Thus the outlaw quest moves **outside** and **beyond**, not **against** the law."[17]

In her book, *Sacred Land, Sacred Sex, Rapture of the Deep*, Dolores La Chapelle shows how children begin to align themselves with nature, by climbing trees and talking to animals. These early experiences with the wild become the basis of developing a life time connection with the land and seeing its sacredness.

SENSUALITY AND ECSTASY

Sensuality and sexuality are deeply hidden in the male shadow. The God Dionysus was quite open with his sensuality, exploring both his masculine and feminine sides. Often he dressed in more effeminate robes and togas, with garlands of ivy on his head. Young boys in our culture are totally discouraged from displaying any womanly qualities whether they be touching, weeping, wearing more feminine clothing, or indulging in fantasy. (It is barely acceptable for young girls to speak with devas or angels, or have imaginary playmates.)

Author Sam Keen speaks about the qualities of maleness in *The Passionate Life*: "the genderal assignments that were grafted onto the biological facts of my maleness taught me some foolish lessons about 'being a real man'. Men don't cry. Control yourself. Be a winner. Real men like Clark Gable, Clint Eastwood, Joe Namath, Alexander Haig, and Ronald Reagan have no self-doubts. They think positively, are always potent, and keep women in their place—which is above men on the pedestal and beneath them in the pecking order and the bedroom."[18]

Children touch their bodies discovering the magic of their various senses. When they try to touch their sexual organs, their hands are slapped and they are told this is "wrong," "bad" or most often "dirty". So sex is quickly perceived as something that must be gotten surreptitiously, in the dark and often **by force.**

As children grow up, they are influenced by films, novels, television. They see that it is okay for men to love youthful, blonde, fair-skinned women, but not okay if the women are dark-skinned, old or ugly. Also not okay if the being is another male. These early programs cause men to place women of other races and cultures, as well as other men, into their bags. What gets placed in the shadow often takes on an outlaw life of its own, becoming an even stronger desire, that goes against the grain of society.

Modern society has become homophobic. Men often avoid friendships with other men as well as hugging and embracing men for fear of being considered queer, weird, or not "real men". They also often avoid friendships with women, especially any physical contact, for fear of what their girl-friends, wives, or neighbors might say. We live in a society where all touching is interpreted as sexual advance or foreplay; the true sensual expression of touching another's body approaches the danger zone.

James Prescott has shown the correlation between child rearing practices, sexual tolerance and physical violence. Societies that provide children with a lot of touching and cuddling, and have a wider range of sensual and sexual options for adults, experience much less interpersonal violence.[19] Prescott's work also reveals studies of child abuse, showing that parents who abuse their children were themselves deprived of physical affection and had an unsatifying sex life.[20]

Our culture condemns nudity in any form; a mother nursing her child in public is frowned upon as are young children running nude on the beach. Yet a huge pornographic industry capitalizes on nude women's bodies, paying huge amounts to the models who pose for the photographs. In her book, ***Pornography and Silence***, Susan Griffin has explored the whole issue of pornography—the abuse and desecration of the sacred body of Woman and the engendering of violence that it catalyzes.

In other cultures, as in India, Woman's body is venerated as the Goddess, the Mother, and is displayed in all art as sensuous and voluptuous. This was also true in the early Neolithic cultures where the Goddess was worshipped. Native and tribal societies have retained the quality of openness in displaying their nudity, and consequently sexuality has not become a perverse, distorted part of life.

So often when children have been deprived of touching and physical nurture, they turn their attention to objects that they try to possess. These objects become more and more important, and their attachment to them becomes greater as they get older. They have transferred their erotic urges to possessions and may at some time in their lives become addicted to those things which provide them the pleasure they never received from loving parents.

"...my body-mind has been deeply informed by the western myth," writes San Keen. "Without second thoughts, I have had a promiscuous affair with machines. Early I lusted after and consummated my desire for a Model A Ford roadster, later a red convertible."

Our culture has not only substituted the possession of things for our erotic encounters with individuals, but the attitude of **possession** has been extended to Women and their sexuality. After the demise of the Goddess cultures, and with the advent of patriarchy, women became objects of possession. They first belonged to their fathers, whose name they took. Later they belonged to their husbands, often sold with a dowry. Their husbands then had the right to own them much as they did their land and servants. Sex became a possessive act, often involving force, rather than a mutual merging of two beings in an ecstatic divine act. Today, many of those beings, women and men, who still understand the sacred function of sex (aside from child bearing) have sought spiritual disciplines as Tantra Yoga or some of the Taoist sexual practices to reclaim the truly erotic and imbue it with spirit.

At the other end of the spectrum is the "sex as conquest" mind set. Sex has often been spoken of in militaristic terms, as though a war were being waged. "The more the identity of the male is rooted in the warrior ideal, the more society will degrade women and cast the relationship between the sexes as a form of warfare, writes author Sam Keene. "The warrior, whether primitive or sophisticated, will see the woman as an inferior to be conquered, raped, dominated."[21]

Sex manuals often use such warfare terminology as a "campaign" to "win a woman or man". Most appalling (and revealing) was the technique, during the Persian Gulf war, of showing pornographic videos to GI's before they set out on a bombing mission. Navy pilots on the U.S.S. Kennedy told an Associated Press reporter they watched pornographic movies before flying bombing runs. [22]In this action we see the ultimate symbolism of the Earth as Woman, who must be raped, overcome and destroyed.

In his essay, "Disarmament and Masculinity", John Stoltenberg discusses the Vietnam war and the men who resisted the draft. "When young males refused to fight in Vietnam, they feebly rebelled against male power over their own lives only to ascertain dominance over the lives of women. They did not have the courage and vision—or perhaps, indeed, the desire—to renounce militarism completely by questioning the institution of patriarchy and by disavowing the cultural power attributed to fathers, in particular fathers' power over sons obtained through the ownership of women's bodies. "[23]

Stoltenberg's point is that we can never have true disarmament until we work out the balance of power between men and women and overturn patriarchy.

"Under patriarchy, normally acculturated males assume—correctly—that the same impulse to sexual violence exists in other males. They therefore endeavor to enter into homoerotic truces—nonaggression pacts contracted between men who tacitly agree to aggress against "others" (women, and sometimes weaker men, or men of other races) instead of one another. When male combat troops do aggress against the territorial rights of other men, their actual military strategy often involves heterosexual rape of the women belonging to those men."[24]

Nowhere has rape and possession been so overwhelming as in the former Yugoslavia where 50,000 Muslim women and young girls have been forced into camps and forcibly raped, according to some accounts as often as 30 times a day.[25] Many of these women were made pregnant by the Serbian soldiers, compounding the horror of rape by giving birth to an unwanted child.

HEALING AND NURTURING THROUGH THE DIONYSUS ARCHETYPE

Dionysus was a nurturer. Bringing the fruit of the vine to people, he represented the Nature Gods, the Green Man. In conducting rituals for his followers, he brought spiritual sustenance. He helped Ariadne when he found her stranded on an island and helped his mother Semele to return from the underworld and ascend to Mount Olympus.

Author Sam Keen writes, "Nowhere is it written in our biological make-up that men may not be tender nor women fierce. ...most rites of initiation are aimed at inculcating sexual specialization and destroying psychological androgyny. Thus men are forbidden to love one half of their nature—that which is soft, intuitive, sensual, bodily, nurturing."[26]

To heal the schism in the psyche between the male and female selves is a deep and ongoing process. As each man works on creating a new balance, so, too, is healing generated between Earth Mother and Sky Father, the earth goddesses and the sky gods. This is reflected in the growing concern for the earth and ecological movements as well as in the seeds now being sown among men who are taking responsibility for rape and abuse of women.

As men begin to explore their "anima" or feminine sides, they feel more connected to their bodies. They are allowing themselves freedom of movement and participating in dance classes, Tai Chi, and other types of sensual movement which allow more flow of energy into the body.

The amount of men undertaking Vision Quests and wilderness trips has doubled in the past few years. Contact with the wild and with one's animal nature rejuvenates and nurtures. It clears out all the cobwebs that have accumulated in the brain and helps reconnect to the feeling center.

The sports men engage in has also changed; less emphasis has been placed on competitive and team sports and more on individual activity, where one uses the body to contact a deeper more intuitive level of being. Running or jogging can be done as meditation; so, too, can skiing which is akin to Tai Chi in its movements. I had a male ski instructor who taught skiing in a transcendental way, and worked with promoting the trance state as a way of achieving a better balance in the body. As one lets go of the mind, the body relaxes and becomes less rigid and more flexible.

Men have also begun to change their appearance since the sixties, with more colorful and looser clothes. Some men have also incorporated jewelry into their dress wearing crystals, beads and earrings. (This is still not acceptable dress in the business community nor in the houses of Congress, but perhaps we will see some loosening of the dress code toward the end of the decade.) Beards and long hair have also become prominent.

Hair suggests a closeness to animals, and therefore those qualities of hot-bloodedness, passion, and spontaneity. (Reptiles, being cold-blooded have no hair.)

RITUAL FOR WORKING WITH THE WILD MAN

Prior to the actual ritual, men should spend time thinking about what it is they want to bring out in their own selves—stronger emotions, deeper passions, developing their intuition. They should also think about what they want to wear, what instruments and other objects they will bring. (Wine and ecstatic drugs should be forbidden, so there is no dependence on outside substances.)

The ritual site should be a special place, preferably outdoors in a wide open area as far away from houses and other people as possible.

Set up a circle with some sort of altar in the center. On this altar place objects representing the four directions as well as other medicine objects, Gods or Goddesses that are special for the men attending. There may also be a picture of Dionysus on the altar if the men desire. Possible ways to demarcate the directions in the center are bird feathers symbolizing East, a candle or some form of fire for South, water in a bowl or pitcher or a shell for West, and a crystal or some cornmeal for North. Other crystals, animal wings or bones, shells and feathers may also be used in decorating the altar.

The place itself and all the participants should be smudged or cleansed with some sort of purifying herb as cedar, sage, sweetgrass, pinon, or other incense.

Before the drumming and music starts, the men should decide who will call in the four directions, Earth Mother and Sky Father, or Goddess and God. One man may play the role of High Priest or several may share it. Wild and ecstatic drumming should start the ritual before the directions and the Gods are invoked.

> *To the East, we call in the golden eagle who*
> *brings in the new day,*
>
> *To the South, we invoke warmth, passion, the god*
> *Shiva in his cosmic dance,*
>
> *To the West, we call in the healing energy and the*
> *black bear that will help us to see and bring out*
> *our wildness,*
>
> *To the North, we call the wisdom of the ancient*
> *ones and the god Dionysus.*

After the directions are called in, each man may share which parts of the God Dionysus he wants to bring out in himself, whether it be related to his passions, intuitive side, work in the world, relationships with others. A good way to conduct the sharing is by passing around a talking stick or other medicine object. (sometimes an Eagle feather which helps to speak the truth may be used.) This allows only one man at a time to speak and helps him to focus his thoughts.

After ending the sharing, each man in turn goes to the middle of the circle and dances out the self he wants to be. It may be helpful to bring a Dionysus mask that each can wear when he dances. While each man dances his wild man, the others drum and rattle, play instruments and chant.

In the third section of the ritual, each person discusses how he felt when dancing and what parts of himself he got in touch with. He may also read a poem or another statement he has written.

To close the ceremony, dance or drum in a totally ecstatic and loose way. When the energy is spent, the spirits of the directions are thanked, one by one, by the men who called them in. Acknowledge the God Dionysus and thank him for his presence. A feast may follow the ritual.

PERSONAL EXPERIENCES WITH THE WILD MAN

BARTON STONE

Growing up in the Bible belt I got lots of messages about the unacceptability of sex and nudity. I knew that allowing girls to see my bare penis would be about the most shameful and disgusting thing I could do, and that they would be filled with embarassment if we boys should even glimpse their underwear. So of course I was fascinated! In groups we made up cruel chants like "I saw London, I saw France, I saw Sally's underpants." The most humiliating trick little boys did was to pull down another's pants in public.

Despite the messages, I still trusted my inner reality. I knew that something that felt so good and interesting could not be all bad. Fortunately I had some close friends, girls and boys, who were also fascinated, and whose prudery was, like mine, mostly social pretense. Our explorations, too furtive to be Dionysian, confirmed my love of bodily pleasures and the thrill of feeling sexual arousal in the company of others.

I also learned the pleasures of solitary sex play and how important it was to keep that hidden because of the shame that would attend discovery.

I realize now that group ecstatic experiences were available then through music and dance. Among my friends social ecstasy was practiced only through the use of alcohol. We had rowdy beer parties and drank ourselves sick.

As I grew older, alcohol produced less ecstasy and more sickness, so I gave it up as a waste of time. My ecstasies became confined to the private sphere, solitary, or with a loved and trusted partner.

A degree of social ecstasy became possible again when I began experimenting with self-generated ritual with friends. We explored ecstatic dance, chanting, all-night singing, drumming, meditation and that particular ecstatic intimacy that sometimes happens when one is in touch with one's most authentic self in sacred time and space.

RICK RAMIREZ

The wild and sensual part of me was repressed when I was growing up due to a strong Catholic upbringing. I was trained to be obedient to the church doctrine and to my parents. However, I personally always enjoyed breaking the rules and confronting authority, especially when I thought it was too rigid.

I started dating girls when I was 6 or 7; I seemed always to be looking for a connection to the female. I would find a girlfriend in my class with whom I would become infatuated. At the age of 7 I was passionately making out with a girl; my mother found out and was really "freaked out".

When I was older, about eleven, I used to explore the sewers, which I found very fascinating and mysterious. Once we ran into a box of girlie magazines in the sewers; this was my first view of the female body and it was very exciting. Because of my upbringing, exploring my wild and sensual side remained a struggle and I tended to do it very secretively.

ENDNOTES:

[1] *Larousse Encyclopedia of Mythology*, p.178.

[2] Ibid., p.179.

[3] Ibid.

[4] Graves, Robert, *The Greek Myths*, vol. 1, p.104.

[5] Ibid., p.180.

[6] Ibid.

[7] Graves, vol. 1, p.110.

[8] Larousse, p.178.

[9] Ibid.

[10] Graves, vol. 1, p.107.

[11] Ibid.

[12] Ibid., p.109.

[13] Bolen, Jean Shinoda, M.D., *Gods in Everyman*, p.255.

[14] Evans, Sir Arthur, *The God of Ecstasy*, p.159.

[15] Ibid., p.160.

[16] Bly, Robert, *Iron John*, p.60

[17] Keene, Sam, *The Passionate Life*, p.130.

Endnotes continued

[18] Ibid., p.144.

[19] Prescott, James, "Body Pleasure and the Origins of Violence," *The Futurist*, April 1975, p.19.

[20] Ibid.

[21] Keene, Sam, p.114.

[22] see "The Sexual Connection," an article by John Gottlieb in *The Progressive*.

[23] Stoltenberg, John, *Refusing to Be a Man*, p.84.

[24] Ibid., p.86.

[25] *Ms*. magazine, Nov.-Dec. 1992, p.11.

[26] Keene, Sam, p.118.

Invocation to the HORNED GOD

Oh Horned One,
Rustling
in the leaves
with the wind.
Circling
the earth
in the birds' wings.
Your energy appears
in the sparks of fire
on a dark night.
We taste your juices
in the ripe corn
and fresh sweet apples.
Pan, Osiris, Tammuz,
God of the changing
earth's rhythmn,
We dance with you
in the moonlight.

The Horned God

Chapter 3

SENSITIVITY AND SACRIFICE—
THE MYTH OF THE HORNED GOD

ost men don't easily open up their channnels of feminine energy. To adopt the "macho" strong man posture is more fashionable and politically safe. Yet there are many men who have never been comfortable with male "machismo"; identifying with the Moon rather than the Sun. Their memories reach back to the time when the Horned God was the consort of the Goddess.

The Horned God is both a hunting god and vegetation god; he is called by many names in various cultures. Where the hunter identified with his prey, he imitated it in acts of sympathetic magic (for example dressing up in the skin of the animal with its horns on his head and doing a ceremonial dance.) Thus the Native Americans worshipped the buffalo; the Minoans revered the bull while in other societies it was the stag or mountain goat.

The Horned God is also the force of Nature who impregnates Mother Earth and is thus responsible for the continuance of the crops and vegetation. He often sacrifices himself to the Earth Mother in the process. Because the idea of sacrifice to a feminine principle is repugnant to most men, it has remained as a part of their shadow.

This sacrifice of the vegetation God was enacted by a human who personified the Corn King. The Corn King was selected for his physical perfection and treated with honor throughout the year. At harvest time he was mated with a priestess who personified the Goddess. Then he was put to death by her or others who participated in the ritual drama.[1]

The shadow side of the Horned God appeared in the Middle Ages when the Church transformed the Horned God into the image of Satan, the devil. From that time on, all horned god figures were thought to represent the forces opposed to the one God. The Horned God became the Anti-Christ. The Inquisition burned those who worshipped any deity with horns. Worshipers of Mother Earth went under cover.

The development of the church coincided with the beginning of technology in Northern Europe. The invention of the heavy plough led to the exploitation of the soils of Northwest Europe and organizations of villages grouped around a church which was its spiritual center and a manor which became the central focus of agriculture.[2] The use of the plough symbolized a new attitude in which people were prepared to wound Mother Earth for their own gain and livelihood.[3] Modern technology with its continuous rape and torture of the Earth has grown from this seed. Christianity was successful in forcing people away from their animistic worship of goddesses and gods of Nature to shrines and artifacts of the saints.

ANCIENT VEGETATION GODS

BAAL

In many traditions, the Horned God served as the son/lover of the

Goddess or Earth Mother. As lover, the God was also the Sun; as son, he was the crops produced by the sacred marriage of Sun and Earth.

One of the earliest vegetation gods was the Canaanite Baal whose story is told in the verses of the Ras Shamra tablets. Baal was the son of the god El and brother of Anat, a fertility goddess and a battle goddess. (In Canaan, agricultural success apparently had to be fought for.) Baal's fertilizing function was bringing rain and thunderstorms to nurture the crops. Baal's enemy was Mot, the god of sterility and death. According to the story, Mot slew Baal. However, before his death, Baal mated with a heifer to assure that the Canaanites would be provided with adequate stock. Baal's sister Anat then traveled to the underworld to recover his body and called for help from Shapash, the Sun Goddess. Afterwards Shapash traveled to the underworld and pleaded unsuccessfully with Mot. So Anat put on her warrior goddess helmet, chopped up Mot with her blade, parched him with fire, ground him up and left him for the birds to eat. Baal was then reborn and the time for rejoicing came again.[4]

OSIRIS

A parallel story set in Egypt features Osiris, the most important god of the Egyptians. On his head he wore a crown with feathers, a solar disk and pair of horns.[5] His body was often colored green suggesting his roles as Corn God and tree spirit. Also known as the Green Man, Osiris taught his people how to make agricultural tools; gather fruit from trees and train the vine to poles.[6] Isis, his sister and queen, who also wears a disk on her head set between horns,[7] discovered wheat and barley and taught the arts of corn-grinding, flax-spinning and weaving.[8]

Osiris was eventually murdered by his jealous brother Set who invited Osiris to lie down in a chest illuminated with suns and stars and inlaid with precious jewels. When Osiris lay down inside, Set and his conspirators nailed down the lid and cast the chest into the Nile. Hearing of this, Isis sheared off a lock of her hair, put on mourning attire and wandered throughout the kingdom in search of the body.[9] Isis used her magic to trace the coffin to the palace of the King of Syria where it had grown into a tree. Given the coffin, she returned home with it and hid it in the Delta only to see Set and his companions find it. They ripped Osiris' body into 14 pieces and scattered them throughout Egypt. Isis found all the pieces except one, the phallus, which she replaced with a golden replica. Apparently, it was a working model because Horus was conceived by Isis and Osiris not long after.[10]

TAMMUZ

One of the very earliest vegetation gods was Tammuz, the Assyro-Babylonian god who was the beloved of Ishtar.[11]

When Tammuz was killed by a boar, Ishtar went to the underworld ruled by her sister Ereshkigal to recover his body. After surrendering a special piece of clothing or jewelry at each of the seven gates of the underworld, she stood naked before her sister, who imprisoned her and afflicted her with illnesses. In the absence of both Ishtar and Tammuz, the earth became barren. Ishtar's father, Sin, the Moon God, and the Sun God Shamash went to Ea, god of wisdom and magic and asked for his help. Ea's messenger traveled to the underworld and cast a magical spell that forced Ereshkigal to release the prisoners, causing the earth to become fertile again.[12]

ADONIS AND ATTIS

The god Adonis, known first in Syria, and later in Greece and Rome, spent part of the year above ground and part in the underworld. Accordingly, he represented the corn or vegetation which lies buried in the earth half the year and reappears above ground the other half.[13]

The mourning ceremony for Adonis was a harvest rite designed to propitiate the Corn God who was either perishing under the sickles or reapers or trodden to death under the hoofs of oxen. While the men slew him, the women wept at home.[14] In early times, Adonis may have been personified by a living man who died a violent death. Among the agricultural societies of the Eastern Mediterranean, Adonis or the corn-spirit was often represented by human victims slain on the harvest field.[15] Adonis' resurrection was seen as the spring plants in bloom again.

In Phrygia, the vegetation god was known as Attis. He was said to be the son of Cybele, an Asiatic goddess of fertility. In the great spring festival of Cybele, the priests slashed parts of their bodies with knives to have their blood flow on the altar; on this same day novices were castrated and their organs buried in the earth.[16]

There are two accounts of Attis' death: in one he was killed by a boar like Tammuz and Adonis; in the other, he castrated himself under a pine treee and bled to death.[17] People grieved for Attis by refusing to eat any bread or flour ground in a mill. This grieving took place in spring, around the vernal equinox. The night before the vernal equinox, Attis' tomb was opened and he rose from the dead. The following day, his resurrection was celebrated with a carnival and festival.[18]

PAN

The goat–footed furry god Pan is the best known of the horned gods. To the Arcadians and early Greeks, he was a god of shepherds and hunting, but as Pan's worship spread geographically, he became identified with blatant sexuality, fertility and music. The Romans merged him with Faunus; the Greeks with Priapus, a phallic fertility god.[19]

Best known for playing his pipes and lasciviously pursuing nymphs in the forest, Pan pursued the gifts of wisdom and prophecy.[20] Connected and in tune with all Nature; his name, Pan, means "all".[21]

HERNE/CERNUNNOS

Herne, an ancient hunting god, is found in old legends and folk tales of Britain. The same god, under the name Cernunnos and Cerne, can be found in Brittany and other parts of France. In this last region, Saint Cornely, the patron saint of horned beasts, is worshipped and depicted in the company of a bull. Portrayed as a giant, he was a great source of fertility. Barren women sat on statues of him (preferably on the phallus) in order to conceive, or wives and husbands had intercourse there. In the enclosure above his head a maypole was set up, a strong symbol of the Horned God's procreative power.

THE HORNED GOD AND THE MALE SHADOW

The Horned God sacrificed himself for the Goddess, for the Earth Mother, to ensure fertility of the land and the growth of crops. He served the earth and when necessary, he gave up his manhood to be of greater service. This memory, service to the female principle, is strong in many men. However, it has not always produced positive experiences because they have felt castrated by their mothers or wives.

There is a distinction between the conscious mother, who is aware of the power she exercises over her son (or daughter) and the unconscious mother who never gives up domination. The young man who is his "mother's son" sees all women as negative mothers whose demands he must try to meet. If he can get in touch with his inner strengths—his sensitivity, spiritual feelings and need for friendship with other men, he can begin to separate actual women from his archetypal projections onto them. In our present culture, so many young boys are brought up solely by their mothers, who have often left dominating and abusive husbands, that they are most aware of female power and may at times feel squelched by it.

Images of Kali, the devouring mother, the all encompassing female, appear and the young boy fights back, adopting a defensive attitude and aligning himself with the "machismo" mode.

Many men, attempting to reclaim the power they lost in their youth, rebel against their mother by abusing other women.

Understanding how the Goddess and God can work together in harmony can take years of therapy as a man works to attain his male/female balance. In his book, *The Horned God—Feminism and Men as Wounding and Healing,* John Rowan shares some important ideas as well as his personal journey to finding the Goddess/female within himself. He speaks of the God as the life force and says that this force is safe and positive when it is united with the Goddess and directed toward the service of life.[22]

The need to feel for men is often experienced as feeling pain, whether that pain is through killing others in wars or through excruciating physical discomfort in sports such as football. Fighting together in a war brings men close together; they experience each other's pain and suffering; likewise, being together on a team brings men into shared emotional experiences where they empathize with each other and go through the highs and lows together. Many men, in writing about their war experiences, recount how much they loved it, how connected they felt to humanity, how exciting the challenge of war was to their spirit. It is sad when men need to kill others in order to feel alive themselves. In his insightful book, *The Trickster, Magician, & Grieving Man*, Glenn Mazis says, "we men need our pain—need to return to the painful Earth in order to rejoin ourselves and others as members of the community 'here'on the planet."[23]

THE HORNED GOD AND PLAYFULNESS

As a God of vegetation, the Horned God had a devic nature (devas are creatures frm the spirit realm who inhabit the earth). He made his way through the fields in the spirit of playfulness; witness the pictures of Pan with his pipe moving gracefully over hill and dale. This light–hearted whimsical quality resides in the male shadow. It is not heroic and is considered fairy–like or feminine. A "real man" must take himself and his work seriously. Humor, however, is a quality needed to balance the seriousness and bring humility into the picture.

A man who can laugh at himself and at the world, who can reverse his direction without blaming himself for making a mistake, is one who walks in balance. Many Native American tribes and other traditonal cultural groups use the concept of the trickster. The trickster (often called coyote or heyokah) intentionally pokes fun at others; he may walk backward or walk in circles. The trickster is not focused on achieving goals, but rather on fooling around, being disorderly and erratic. He does not approach life through his ego and thus is open and vulnerable in his dealings with others. For men to agree to play with the trickster, they must sacrifice their sense of self or ego and allow themselves to become vulnerable. As a result, they will let go of old ways of approaching problems and the expectations of others. This catalyzes their own creativity and humor while broadening their life experience.

RITUALS FOR THE HORNED GOD

Before the first ritual, each man should consider his vulnerability. He should recall how he has been hurt or torn apart by others or by society. He might also think about whether he has defended the earth, or whether for reasons of keeping his livelihood or his friends, he has knowingly contributed to the desecration of the earth. Another area to examine is the relationship between his own inner male and inner female. Are they in balance? Does he have a well developed inner female that nurtures him, or does he look outside of himself for this?

Prepare a space for the ritual, cleansing it with cedar, sage, or incense. If possible, this ritual should be held outdoors under the sky near natural elements—trees, rocks, plants, birds and animals.

The altar should have animal parts and feathers symbolic of the Horned One plus the gifts from the Earth Mother—grains, herbs, vegetables and fruits of the season since the horned god is a vegetation god.

In the East, various bird feathers may be placed to represent the element air. The feathers of birds who are known for their medicine power should be used, as eagle, hawk and owl though care should be taken as to who is attending the ritual since these feathers are considered illegal in the United States. (unless one has papers allowing him/her to carry the feather.)

In the South, a candle is used to symbolize fire as well as any other symbols that suggest the fire and passion of the South. The West is the place of water, intuition, and the home of the black bear. Shells and a chalice of water may be placed here; also bear claws or any other parts of the bear.

As the North is the place of wisdom, the elders, and the land of the buffalo, antlers from a deer or stag may be put here to represent the elders of the animal kingdom as well as any representations of the buffalo. Crystals may also be placed in the North to represent the earth.

In calling in the directions, the various horned gods are used.

> *To the East, we call in Tammuz, ancient god of the earth and the plants,*

> *To the South, we call in Pan, shepherd god of Arcadia, with his pipes and music,*

> *To the West, we call in Osiris, Egyptian god of the Underworld,*

> *To the North, we call in Herne/Cernunnos to bring us the wisdom of the elders.*

In the first part of the ritual Osiris is the focus. Men in the circle share how they have been torn apart by society or by other men and women. They then speak of their healing and how they have re-integrated their pieces, including their creative and fertile power.

In the second part of the ritual the sharing is on the Earth Mother—how the earth has been raped and abused and what can be done to heal her.

Balancing the inner male and inner female through the god and goddess is the focus of the third section. Each man shares how he is working to create this balance.

Finally, Pan is invoked and the feeling is one of celebration as musical instruments are played and songs shared for the healing and the coming together of god and goddess.

After the ritual, celebrate the vegetation god by feasting on maize or cornbread, squashes, green vegetables, salads and seasonal fruit.

RITUAL FOR THE TRICKSTER

In the second ritual, the altar is prepared as above, but there might be pictures of various trickster figures, the Fool card from the Tarot deck, the heyokah or clown.

After the four directions are called in, the spirit of the trickster is also invoked. He may be invoked as the Fool, the coyote, or as heyokah.

In the first part of the ritual, the men circle backwards, playing rattles, drums, and other instruments. They may break out of the circle and move in different directions, dancing or spinning through space.

In the second part, each man plays the trickster, one at a time. He may confront one of the other men or several men and evoke their responses. After all the men have played trickster, they resume their places in the circle and share how they felt, both as the trickster and as the one confronted. What part of them felt vulnerable? What part enjoyed the humor?

The ritual closes with songs and Pan-like dancing, after which there may be feasting.

MEN'S EXPERIENCES WITH THE HORNED GOD

BARTON STONE

After years of living in metropolitan areas and pursuing metropolitan struggles, I found myself on the ocean side of Mount Tamalpais, a beautiful sacred mountain across the Golden Gate from San Francisco. The coastal hills are still quite wild there with oak and hay woodlands, chaparral, and redwood trees along the creeks and canyons.

I was having a mid-life crisis, profoundly questioning my identity and purpose. I sought comfort in the wild plants and animals of the area, learned the names and qualities of many of them, and felt an excitement and an acceptance as if I had entered a new community and was just getting acquainted with fascinating new neighbors.

On familiar trails I developed a personal relationship with individual plants and followed their progress through their cycles. Natural features of individual plants and animals such as a rock outcropping, a canyon, a grove of bushes became as real and important to me as personal human relationships.

Suddenly I began seeing great horned owls, especially a pair in whose territory I had been living. The huge owls impressed me with the power of a revelation. After the first time, I began seeing them often, at any hour. I learned their favorite roosts and their calls. I learned to tell them apart. Sometimes they responded to my imitation of their calls hoot for hoot. Whether this was in appreciation or derision, I couldn't tell, but I felt a joy of discovery in entering their world that was deeply moving and sustaining to me.

I found that my true nature is earth within earth, a wild thing among wild things, and this is thrilling.

RICK RAMIREZ

Since the time I was a young child, I've always had a deep attraction for Nature and the powerful energies of animals. When I was about three or four, I started to ride horses in Puerto Rico, where I spent my summers. I felt exultant being on this powerful animal. My childhood hero was Tarzan; I admired his intuitive connection with nature and animals. I loved the film *Greystone* where he turned his back on wealth and retired to the jungle. I think the Tarzan myth is one of the great myths of our era.

My grandfather was a farmer; his land was like the jungle and certainly different from Baltimore! The people who worked on the farm were close to Nature; they had Indian blood in them and were very poor, eking out a living through their simple work. I felt a strong kinship with these people who worked with their hands on the earth.

My father, on the other hand, felt that a professional person should not dirty his hands. His way of gardening was very different and I couldn't relate to it. This was a very tense issue between us.

When my Dad taught me how to ride a horse, he showed me how to be real firm and always in control. This was how I learned, to be in control of the animal rather than being one with the animal, which felt better to me.

ENDNOTES

[1] Farrar, Janet & Stewart, *The Witches God*, p.23.

[2] Anderson, William, *Green Man*, p.50.

[3] Ibid.

[4] Farrar, Janet & Stewart, pp.21–23.

[5] Richardson, Alan, *Earth God Rising*, p.5.

[6] Frazer, Sir James George, *The Golden Bough*, p.421

[7] Isis was often identified with Hathor, the cow goddess in Egypt, who originated from another tradition

[8] Richardson, p.7.

[9] Ibid.

[10] Ibid., pp.9,10,11.

[11] Until the beginning of the second milennium B.C. Tammuz was known as Dumuzzi, the consort of Inanna. He is also the antecedent of the Phoenician Adoni as well as the Syrian and later Greek Adonis.

[12] Farrar, p.87.

[13] Frazer speaks of the corn being underground which apparently refers to some type of grain because corn as we know it originated in the New World. See Frazer, pp.390–392.

[14] Frazer, p.393.

[15] Ibid.

[16] Frazer, p.405.

[17] Ibid., p.404

[18] Ibid., p.407.

[19] Ibid.

[20] .Farrar, p.77.

[21] In *Earth God Rising,* Alan Richardson suggests that Pan and his ilk are comparable to the man-beast who guards the portals of the underworld. The horned god and his consort have concerns with the land, its significance in human consciousness, and what lies below it. See *Earth God Rising,* p.82.

[22] Rowan, John, *The Horned God,* p.86.

[23] Mazis, Glen, *The Trickster, Magician, & Grieving Man, Reconnecting Men with Earth,* p.47.

Invocation to HEPHAESTUS

Oh Hephaestus,

lame but valiant,

rejected by Hera,

deceived by Aphrodite.

Dwelling in the depths

of the underground,

with your forge and smithy,

Making awesome objects,

thrones and thunderbolts.

Oh Hephaestus,

Share your creative spirit,

and your strong will.

Hephaestus

Chapter 4

CREATIVITY, HEALING AND REJECTION BY MOTHER— THE MYTH OF HEPHAESTUS

reativity in its deepest sense has never been considered a masculine trait though there are many male artists, writers, photographers, musicians, actors and dancers. Women have always been known as the creators because of their ability to birth new life. Women are also thought to be more receptive and intuitive, traits associated with the creative process. Throughout the ages men have been stereotyped as "breadwinner", whether they left home to hunt game, or commuted to an office earning money for their families.

Men's desire to study art, writing or music has usually been frowned on by society. Consequently, those desires are usually held back, forced underground until the dam breaks (often catalyzed by intense emotional events) and the creative juices pour forth. It is at this point that many men connect with their deeper selves and become rebellious toward the demands of family and society. They may adapt a different lifestyle, one that is exciting and colorful but more stringent economically. At various times such men who have rejected demands of family and society have been called bohemian, beatnik and hippie.

Although a few well–known artists, writers, musicians and craftsmen earn rich rewards for their work, most find it necessary to maintain some more remunerative way to earn money and fulfill their creativity during evening or week-end hours. Even if one's creative output does not bring financial wealth, personal fulfillment, empowerment and sense of self-worth is extremly important.

A key element in the creative process is the catalyst—a joyous, painful, or intense emotion that must be expressed. Loss of a family member or loved one, separation, rejection, the birth of a child, the coming together or marrying of two individuals are all personal events that prompt artistic expression. Worldwide catastrophes and political events may also trigger feelings that catalyze the creative process. So, too, does an appreciation of the beauties of nature—seeing a rainbow in the sky or a spectacular sunset.

More often than not, however, men's feelings, whether of joy or pain, are not shared but stuffed into that bag called the shadow, the unconsious reservoir where so many of our gut reactions are buried. There they fester and stagnate, often leading to physical problems or emotional disorders. At this point a man needs to open up the bag, examine the wounds, and begin a process of self-healing.

The myth of Hephaestus, or Vulcan as he was known in Rome, is an extremely dynamic one for working with the male shadow. Hephaestus, who was born lame, was thrown off Mount Olympus, rejected by his mother Hera and also by his father Zeus. Through his art of metalsmithing, he brought beauty to the world and also healed himself. But when he married Aphrodite (Venus), her sexual liaison with Ares (Mars), brought him ridicule and wounded him yet again. Thus, within the myth Hephaestus, we have the prototype of male creative and healing energy as well as rejection by mother and cuckolding by wife, all important elements in the male shadow.

MYTH OF HEPHAESTUS

Hephaestus, the son of Hera and Zeus, was born lame in both legs, with twisted feet and a dislocated hip. Hera tried to hide him from the other Olympians by throwing him into the sea where he was adopted by Thetis, daughter of Nereus, and Eurynome, daughter of the old Ocean. For nine years he remained concealed in their grotto, forging objects for the nymphs and planning his revenge. He made Hera a golden throne with great artistry. When the goddess sat on it and tried to get up, she was gripped by invisible bands. The Olympians could not extricate her from the throne. When Hephaestus refused to leave the ocean to help her, Ares tried to drag him back but Hephaestus threw burning irons at him. Dionysus finally made him drunk and brought him to Olympus. Hephaestus agreed to set Hera free, but only if he could have the loveliest goddess, Aphrodite, for his bride.[1]

Eventually, Hephaestus made peace with Hera and defended her when Zeus beat her. Zeus, however, became irritated with him and flung him from Olympus to the volcanic island of Lemnos, the place where the cult of Hephaestus originated.[2]

Hephaestus was a master of metal work. He built palaces for the gods, made Zeus' throne and thunderbolts, the winged chariot of Helios, the arrows of Apollo and Artemis and other fine works. He split Zeus' skull when he gave birth to Athena and bound Prometheus to the Caucasus.[3]

Despite his deformity, Hephaestus had many loves. He was the husband of Aphrodite, though she was constantly unfaithful to him. At one point Hephaestus imprisoned his wife and Ares in a net and exposed them to ridicule by the Olympians. Although infatuated with Athena, she continously spurned his advances. Others accepted him, however, for he is said to have married both Charis and Aglaia, one of the Graces, as well as fathering the Cabeiri (underground smiths of Lemnos who were seen as benevolent geniis) with Cabeiro and the Palici, the Dioscuri of Sicily, with the Oceanid Etna.[4]

MYTH OF HEPHAESTUS AND THE MALE SHADOW

Hephaestus was rejected in a culture of the sky gods where power, heroism, and physical appearance were revered. This Olympian culture was perhaps the first prototype of patriarchal societies in which the earth and elements of the earth have been devalued. There Hephaestus with his underground workshop and forge was an outlaw. He literally used the element of fire to transform his feelings and forge creative work. Fire or passion allows us to transmute feelings of rejection or betrayal into works of art and to heal ourselves in the process. Literally and figuratively, Hephaestus is an archetypal myth for the creative process.

Jean Shinoda Bolen relates that subterranean fire is a metaphor for passionate feelings that are contained within our bodies until expressed.[5] The Hephaestus type tends to sublimate his feelings and express them through some creative project. He does not share or discuss these feelings but rather seethes with emotion, using it to fuel his artistry.

The creation of a piece of art or material object enhances the creator's sense of self-esteem. And, like Hephaestus, the artist may become so celebrated for his work that attention is no longer paid to his physical or emotional deformity. Examples of this were the artist Van Gogh who cut off his ear in a fit of passion and later painted himself with a bandaged ear, creating a work of art from his suffering. Toulouse Lautrec was, in fact, lame like Hephaestus but became a painter of high regard in his time. The musician Chopin suffered deep emotional passions which he transformed into his music while Beethoven who was deaf, composed strongly emotional music. Eugene O'Neill revealed the depths of his troubled soul through his plays and F. Scott Fitzgerald portrayed his difficult marriage in his novels.

Rejection by the mother will influence the rest of a man's life unless he undergoes deep therapy and understands his mother's psychological make-up as well as his relationship with her. Why was it necessary for her to reject him? Men who fail to do this necessary therapeutic work may have lasting problems with women, repeatedly rejected by those to whom they are emotionally and sexually attracted. A man who has consistently tried to please his mother in vain becomes resentful. By connecting with his real feelings, he can stop seeing all women as "negative mothers" whose demands he is trying to accomodate.[6]

Today many single mothers are responsible for their children's livelihood and their nurturing. The pressure can become unbearable, leading to both neglect and abuse. When such mothers have little life experience and no opportunity or time to heal their own wounds (as is the case with teenage mothers), these patterns of neglect and abuse are passed on to their children and the cycle continues.

The early death or desertion of a mother is another type of neglect. When a young boy never receives the nurturing from the female, he spends most of his life looking for it.

Most common, however, in mother-son relationships is the dominating mother, or over-powering mother. This pattern usually starts very early when the mother places her needs over those of her child and sees him as an extension of herself. Such a son never gets to find his "core self" or to express his own opinions or feelings unless he rebels against his mother and leaves her. This is often the case in adolescence when boys join gangs or groups where male power is displayed. Drugs, theft and violence are negative ways of rebelling against the mother. A more positive approach is for the young boy to take off on his own, to travel, study and explore life, thereby finding his own soul. This parallels ancient vision quest and male initiation.

Male rituals, which are held in all tribal societies, are not just about being separated from mother and mother's protection. They are about a boy's acquiring his personal power, becoming a "warrior" in the sense of learning to protect himself in a harsh environment, and finding out who he really is. This involves a time of meditation and contemplation so that he may connect with his soul and true essence. Various tribes have different types of initiation rituals; some involve the boy's survival in the wilderness with primitive weapons for hunting and protection. Others involve vision quests at places of power where the boy can develop his psychic faculties and attune to the spirits of animals, birds, ancestors and others who may be guides for him. In certain South American tribes, psychotropic medicinal plants are used, enabling the initiate to access the spirit world and understand how to navigate in the higher realms.

Another aspect of the mother-son relationship is the three–fold relationship between mother, father and son. This triangular relationship can take many forms. Once Hephaestus bonded and healed the wounds with his mother, he protected her against his father. Often a male child sees himself as his mother's protector, especially when there is an abusive, delinquent or alcoholic father. The myth of Oedipus, who killed his father and married his mother (not realizing she was his mother), provides another archetype. How many young men, in fact, desire to kill their fathers so that they may become the head of the household and protector of mother? How many young men are forced into this role because of a father's death or abandonment of the household?

Only when there is a harmonious relationship between mother and father can the son receive nurturing from both and not pit one against the other. Too often, in broken households, the mother speaks badly of the father or the father denigrates the mother so that the son is filled with negatives about both his parents. This leads to confusion, taking sides, and subsequently a loss of his own power when he spends his early adult years seeking the nurturing he never received. This situation can become complicated when one of the parents re-marries or has a new partner. The son's allegiance to his original parents may conflict with his ability to receive love from the surrogate parent. Unless he finds good role models for both the female and male energies that he craves, he is likely to become a confused adolescent and adult.

Sam Keen speaks of the need for us to re-experience our anger and resentment against our parents. In doing this, we free ourselves of dependence and obedience and in time, understand, forgive and experience compassion.[7] We have all been wounded in childhood, but we have the ability to heal ourselves and transform those wounds. This may be through physical creations such as works of art or at the soul level, where we learn to recognize beauty and exhibit the same compassion to others that we manifest toward ourselves. To be healed we must return to our woundedness. To become powerful we must experience our impotence.

RITUAL FOR WORKING WITH CREATIVITY

Our first ritual brings our creative spirit out into the open. The group performing the ritual needs to meet twice, once for the preliminary ritual and a second time for sharing creative projects that emerge out of the ritual. If the group meets regularly, these rituals can be the basis of two meetings.

When the ritual is performed indoors, a large space is needed where there is room to move. Be sure the entire space is smudged and blessed before setting up an altar and the circle. On the altar place some personal ritual implements as well as pictures of Hephaestus or Vulcan. As explained in previous chapters, there should also be a ritual object to demarcate each of the four directions.

To purify each participant, pass a smudge bowl or abalone shell with cedar, sage, sweetgrass, or some incense to symbolize the fire of creativity. During the smudging and afterwards, the men will drum and rattle to bring out as much passion and feeling as possible. The directions are called in by the man leading the ritual or by several men.

> *To the East, I call in the golden eagle and ask for a cycle of new beginnings, that we may express our creative energy just as the Sun rises each day.*

> *To the South, I call in the fire and passion of Hephaestus, that we may feel our fire and manifest it.*

> *To the West, I call in the shadows of evening and dusk, the dark places where healing occurs. I call in the black bear who helps us to heal ourselves and nurture others.*

> *To the North, I call in the ancient wisdom of the grandmothers and grandfathers who bring us the truth of our creative spirit.*

The talking stick is passed and each man shares how he has expressed his creative energy or where he feels blocked. After the sharing, the drums, rattles and instruments are placed in the center of the circle. The men begin to dance in a circle, each one expressing his own needs without regard to the others. At any point, a man may pick up a drum or instrument and play it. The intention is to allow energy to flow through the body and to facilitate the emergence of animal spirits or any feelings that may arise. (During this time lights are turned out and only candles lit.)

When all have completed their dance/movement, a small light may be turned on. The men return to their places in the circle and share what they have experienced. The circle is then completed with chants or songs.

The second ritual provides follow–up on the first. This time the altar may be decorated with things the men themselves have made, whether art or ritual objects. Smudging and calling in of directions is done as before, but each person now shares a poem, story or an object he has created as a result of the first ceremony and prays for this creative spirit to continue to move through him. At the end of the ceremony, there is a general celebration with singing, dancing, and feasting.

RITUAL FOR CLEARING ENERGY WITH MOTHER

This should be done first as an individual ritual with the assistance of a person who is trained in counseling or higher energy work. Once the room and both participants are smudged, the person who is working on clearing lies down in a relaxed fashion on a mat. The facilitator uses color meditation or another visualization exercise to induce the participant into a deep state of consciousness. The facilitator then guides the participant in calling in his authentic or spiritual self and the spiritual self of his mother. The participant speaks of his hurts, sorrows, disappointments and anger to his mother's authentic self. After releasing these, he may cry and become very emotional. If he feels ready at this point, he can forgive his mother and send her love.

After this ritual, the individual should write in his journal, or write a letter to his mother, which serves as a vehicle for releasing his feelings furthur. It does not matter in doing this whether his mother is alive or not; this letter need not be sent.

Another exercise to be done later also involves the help of a trained facilitator. After calling in the spiritual selves, the participant cuts the cords between himself and his mother and clears the chakras.

GROUP RITUAL

An altar is built and the group smudged as before. Various goddesses who portray parts of the feminine may be called on with the four directions.

> To the East, we call in Athena, goddess of the air element, who brings us new beginnings in dealing with the feminine,
>
> To the South, we call in Pele, goddess of fire, who fills us with the passions and emotions of the feminine,
>
> To the West, we call in Inanna, she who represents water and goes into the lower depths to connect with her shadow,
>
> To the North, we call in Demeter, Earth Mother, to bring us the wisdom and nurture of the feminine.

Each man in the circle shares his relationship with his mother and how it has affected and influenced his life. One by one, each takes a turn in clearing this energy, speaking with his mother, letting out anger, crying, or thanking her for how she has helped.

The leader or High Priest then talks about male wounding, and how each man has been wounded in his life. He speaks about the idea of perfection, citing that none is perfect and that all are wounded.

Next all share the nature of their relationships with other women in their lives, how they have been helped or wounded. Each may need to clear the energy with individual females. If the group has more than four or five men, this part should be done as a separate ritual since it is important for each man to have time to clear and work with each female whom he feels has wounded him. If the ritual is done over a week-end, one day could be devoted to processing with mother and one day for working with other women.

After the ritual, there is singing and celebrating.

PERSONAL EXPERIENCES WITH HEPHAESTUS ARCHETYPE

BARTON STONE

Though I was personally blessed to be born to a birth mother who was present, loving and attentive throughout my childnood, culturally I grew up in a house without a mother. It was a Protestant Christian household, a milieu presided over by the Heavenly Father (with my own father's help). No Heavenly Mother mediated His remoteness and paternalistic judgement. Religious language and imagery was almost entirely male and religious icons were scorned as idolatrous.

After years of atheism in reaction to that dryness, my experiences in wild nature led me to investigate religious systems which acknowledge nature spirits—Shamanism, Shinto and Wiccan ways. Mother Nature, Mother Earth, began to come forth into my consciousness like water from an ancient spring.

Awed by the representations of Her produced in the old Paleolithic period, before the practice of agriculture, I began to fashion ceramic replicas of the "Venuses" of Willendorf and Lausel. My whole heart and body responded in relief to these little figurines.

Later I started to visualize more about who She was and to make altarpieces and Goddess icons that could restore an image of God the Mother for others like me who longed for the feminine divine. I carved stone figurines of feminine power, authority, and wisdom as well as nurturance and beauty. There are images of the great serpent mother and the mother of tigers. There are mother bears, fiercely protective of their children and mother owls, at home in the dark. The Queen of Heaven weaves the stars and their influences, and the Tooth Mother makes way for the new by gobbling the old. There are priestesses who speak for the animal nations among the councils of humans and who attend the sick and dying.

These figures are still not socially acceptable. Many see them as some kind of exotic cult paraphernalia or as art objects that might be part of a room decor. Their content might seem primitive or embarassing. However, they are just a small part of a large re-visioning of our most basic beliefs. I believe they will play their part in the collective dream we are dreaming, which will surely gather reality over time, helping us find a way to balance and redeem the masculine excesses of the past five millenia.

RICK RAMIREZ

I was confused about my mother's love when I was young because she had injured her hip in giving birth to me and was put in a full body cast. For the first six months of my life, I was apart from her—first with one grandmother in New York and then with my father's mother in Puerto Rico. I never really bonded with my mother and this impacted on my intimate relationships throughout my life. Actually, it wasn't until I was thirty five that I found out what had truly happened; she used to tell me that she fell on the ice or some such story.

The Hephaestus myth is really attractive to me because it speaks of an alchemical process—working with fire and base metals. I feel that my uncovering of knowledge in myself has been a kind of alchemical process and a way of working through my own tension of rejection.

In terms of creativity, my strongest relationship was with music. My mother played beautiful Chopin waltzes and I began piano lessons at the age of seven or eight. My father also loved classical music and I remember conducting Beethoven's Fifth Symphony in my living room. Music for me was my own therapy, a way of expressing something very deeply, not so much a craft but a personal outlet. More recently, acting and story-telling have been creative modes of expression that satisfy me, particuarly when I can combine story-telling with music.

ENDNOTES

[1] *Larousse Encyclopedia of Mythology*, p.139.

[2] Ibid.

[3] Ibid., p.140.

[4] Ibid.

[5] Bolen, Jean Shinoda, M.D., *Gods in Everyman*, p.223.

[6] Woodman, Marion, *The Pregnant Virgin*, p.157.

[7] Keen, Sam, *The Passionate Life*, p.211.

Invocation to ARES

Fiery Ares,

raging into battle,

brandishing your sword,

Fiery Ares,

racing into love—making,

brandishing your penis,

impulsive,

strong willed,

courageous,

loyal.

Ares

Chapter 5

THE MALE WARRIOR—
THE MYTH OF ARES

arrior, a term that is most often mis-understood in our society, takes on a new dimension when it is related to the male shadow. What is a true warrior and why are men (and women too) afraid to show this part of themselves to society?

To many in our culture a warrior is one who goes to war, who takes up arms against his enemy. He may therefore be chastised for the act of killing or applauded for defending his race, religion, country, or tribe. In contrast, tribal societies urge a young man to undergo initiation in order to develop the warrior traits of courage, endurance, decisiveness, good judgment, and wisdom. A warrior must be able to decide quickly when it is wise to run for cover and when it is better to take his knife or sword and engage his enemy. To survive in the wilderness a warrior must be able to gather edible plants, hunt game, make a shelter, and keep warm. All this demands connection with the spiritual energy of the universe so that he will be guided in all his actions and not motivated by fear.

When warrior energy is suppressed, it can erupt violently like a volcano. Men who hold unfulfilling low paying menial jobs as well as those who have given over their power to a boss or manager, often reach a boiling point. Frustration and anger can lead to crazy and irrational behavior as well as violence to self and others.

Warriors have played a role in world history for eons. In ancient India, the *kshatriya* clan protected its land and helped spread its civilization throughout Asia. In Egypt, the Pharoahs established large armies with which to fight their neighbors and protect their civilization. The Spartans, warriors of ancient Greece, fought the Persians. And the Roman emperors organized huge armies which conquered much of Europe. In North America, Native American tribes warred among themselves long before the white men came on to the scene.

This historical perspective raises several questions: How much of man's war–like nature is biological and genetic? How much is a societal function that arises once a group is formed and needs to protect itself? How much is an evolutionary necessity to spread culture and civilization?

War–like tribes replaced agricultural societies in the age of Ares (2300 BCE–0 BCE). For farmers in agricultural societies, life was a struggle that required working with nature and constantly flowing with her cycles. In the age of Ares, there were myths relating to the ram and to the Rama empire in India; this material is found in the Hindu epics, the **Ramayana** and **Mahabarata**. With the advent of warrior societies, the struggle shifted away from nature toward other humans. Men stopped obeying nature's cycles and declared their individual power over her. The individual being took on more importance than the tribe or social group. In the process, Mother Earth and women slipped into subordinate positions. A by–product of these warring tribes was the spread of civilization and exchange of goods and information.

As author Sam Keen puts it, "The quest for harmony was replaced by the search for control. The dominance of the senses was replaced by the discipline of willpower. The realm of the sacred was no longer to be found in the nearby fields, rivers, and glades, but in the remote heavenly dwelling of the transcendent God. The business of God was more in the realm of politics than agriculture. He was better at commanding his people to go on crusades and sanctifying genocide than he was at dancing round the maypole or growing crops."[1]

Through studying certain of the Japanese martial arts as aikido, we can gain insights into the manifestation of warrior consciousness. Training in aikido involves the balance of heart, mind, and body. Skills are aimed at protecting the individual and developing his courage. The object is not to wound the opponent but only to thwart his attack. An example of a true warrior is Carlos Castaneda's Don Juan, a sorcerer and magician who manifests the warrior qualities of courage, power, endurance and centeredness.

The true warrior is motivated by a cause beyond himself. Acting as a transpersonal *tour de force*, he goes out into the world to serve his country, his king, his tribe or his religion. Modern soldiers, however, have rarely completed spiritual warrior training and typically act from obedience to a higher authority or from fear of losing their lives. Few of today's soldiers possess emotional maturity or understanding. Bombing, shelling, killing innocent civilians and torturing the enemy are not part of the warrior path; they stem from the shadow side of the warrior. When there are victims on one side, there can be **no** true warriors on the other, but only emotionally damaged men who are interested in POWER OVER others, men out of touch with their power within. Warrior energies gone amok lead to sadistic tendencies as revealed in the Holocaust and Hitler's SS. Sadists eradicate those whom they consider vulnerable and weak in society—witness the recent action by a neo–Nazi group in Germany who carved a swastika on the cheek of a young woman in a wheelchair. Sadism as practiced in this way covers up the weak vulnerable places in the psyche and temporarily makes the individual or group feel powerful. This same pattern has been present in the rape camps of Bosnia–Herzogovina. Men afraid of their own passive female violate women to gain the illusion that they have conquered that weakness within themselves.

In their book, *King, Warrior, Magician, Lover,* Robert Moore and Douglas Gillette speak of the "Shadow Warrior." "The Shadow Warrior carries into adulthood the adolescent insecurity, violent emotionalism, and the desperation of the Hero as he seeks to make a stand against the overwhelming power of the feminine, which always tends to evoke the masochistic or cowardly pole of the Hero's dysfunctional Shadow. The man under the influence of the Shadow Warrior's bipolarity, unsure of his phallic power, is still battling against what he experiences as the inordinately powerful feminine and against everything supposedly 'soft' and relational. Even in adulthood he still feels terrified that he will be swallowed up by it. His desperate fear thus leads him to wanton brutality."[2]

Yet another "Shadow Warrior" is the revolutionary who overthrows the tyrannical ruler only to take on the role himself. Real warriors uphold their own truth, regardless of society's support, and are willing to walk alone. Mahatma Ghandi and Martin Luther King embody warrior consciousness in action.

In *Care of the Soul,* Thomas Moore refers to the ancient myth of Ares/Mars. "Renaissance doctors placed both anger and the life force under the aegis of one god, Mars. All people, they taught, have an explosive force ready within them to be unleashed into the world. Simply being oneself—letting one's individuality and unique gifts come forth—is a manifestation of Mars. When we allow ourselves to exist truly and fully, we **sting** the world with our vision and challenge it with our own ways of being."[3]

MYTH OF ARES

"Of all the gods who live on Olympus, thou art the most odious to me; for thou enjoyest nothing but strife, war and battles," said Zeus of his son Ares in the Iliad. "Thou hast the obstinate and unmanageable disposition of thy mother Hera, whom I can scarcely control with my words."[4]

As a boy, Ares was almost killed by the giant sons of Aloeus who placed him in a jar for thirteen months, a punishment that surely did not improve his battling disposition.[5]

On a more positive note, Hera chose the phallic god Priapus as Ares' tutor so that he would train Ares to be a perfect dancer, warrior and lover.

Impetuous, brutal, and hotheaded, Ares constantly warred against Athena who represented courage and coolness. In the Trojan war, fighting on the side of the Trojans against the Greeks, Ares fought for men with whom he was bound by blood or loyalty.

Ares fell in love with Aphrodite, wife of Hephaestus, and together they had three children—Deimos (Fear) and Phobos (Panic) who accompanied Ares on the battlefield, and Harmonia, whose name suggests the harmony between her parents' great passions, love and war.[6] Hephaestus, who was not pleased by her adventuring, fashioned a hunting net that could not be seen, attached it to the sides of his marriage bed and brought in all his Olympian friends to watch Ares and Aphrodite when they became helplessly entangled in lust.[7]

After discovering that Aphrodite philandered with Adonis, Ares turned himself into a wild boar and gored his rival to death.[8]

Besides his children with Aphrodite, Ares fathered nearly twenty others through various liaisons. Three of his sons were Argonauts and one of his daughters was the Amazon queen Penthesileia.[9]

MYTH OF ARES AND THE MALE SHADOW

The myth of Ares brings out many of the characteristics that are found in the shadow side—impetuosity, emotionality, rage, lust for battle and lust for women. The Ares archetype represents braun not brains and has often been associated with athletes and others who are robust physically but lacking in refinement or verbal agility. Even Zeus denounced his son for being too physical and acting without forethought.

On the positive side, Jean Shinoda Bolen points out in her book, *Gods in Everyman,* that Ares was a protector who saved his daughter and his sons. Later, as the Roman god Mars, he became the protector of the city of Rome.[10] Loyal to his friends, he protected them in battle when he was able.

Rejected by his father, Ares went on to be rebuffed by Athena, the archetype of the intellectual woman. He was accepted by women like Aphrodite, however, who were aroused by his physical and sexual prowess.

Few married men ever trusted him; aware of his adulterous and lusty love affairs, they feared he would disrupt their committed relationships with women.

WORKING WITH THE SHADOW AS SEEN IN THE ARES MYTH

ANGER AND RAGE

The myth of Ares reflects male anger which often leads to abuse, both physically and emotionally. It is also related to the shadow in its portrayal of male sexuality and rejection by the father.

Anger at another human being or at society when not channeled and used constructively, can lead to rage, an uncontrollable emotion that produces violent and abusive acts.

Most individuals who experience anger do not know how to work with it. To work with it is to understand its source, whether the anger is directed at another person or at oneself, because anger is so often related to frustration. When we are not clear in our boundaries with others, we often get angry with them. We might feel that they are taking advantage of us in some way, or not being considerate of us, when, in actuality, it is we who need to state what our boundaries are and what we will or will not tolerate. This is particualry common where a strong angry parent has scared the child at an early age and the child, even grown up, is too fearful to confront the parent. He repeatedly becomes angry at the parent until the anger turns into rage. Once he is raging, he is out of control and is capable of physically hurting the parent. This may have been the scenario in the case of the Melendez brothers in Southern California who shot both their parents. They contend that the parents had been physically and sexually abusive for so long that they feared for their own lives.

Rage can also be paralyzing and lead to severe depression. Those who are unable to take any action against their abuser, yet are consumed by rage, may stop their routine activities and become more and more withdrawn and depressed.

Physical activity and creative projects, along with therapy, can help to move the energy. Those who are depressed disconnect from fire energy which is both physical and creative. Running, dancing, swimming, yoga and all other forms of physical exercise stoke the fires. Writing, painting, sculpting, making pottery, drumming and playing an instrument are all ways that help to express rage and release it. As a friend of mine once said, "It is better to make a pot than break a pot."

Working in therapy individually or in groups is important to access the source of anger and rage. Men who see the patterns from family and childhood can change them and clear the energy with the individuals. This may be done verbally or silently through visualization and meditation if the other people are not receptive to changing the pattern.

SEXUALITY

The Ares archetype includes unbridled sexuality, often brutal and abusive. It contrasts with the sensuality represented by Dionysus and the wild man. For Ares, sexuality and war are intricately related; both arise from strong passions and the desire for conquest. There is little concern or consideration for the other individual, group or nation. In the chapter on Dionysus, I related the story about the American soldiers watching pornographic films before they went on bombing missions during the Persian Gulf war. Capturing and forcing women to submit to them was the incentive for bombing the "enemy", often poor civilians.

The origins of this type of sexuality lie in the invasion of the Aryan tribes and the culture of the transcendent Sky Father whose sperm was capable of subjugating the feminine. Women assumed the procreative maternal role and became subordinates while sexuality was reduced to a biological act.

Sensuality and sexuality are much broader than genital sex. Taoist and Tantric literature reveal practices which retain the semen using it to nourish the whole body. Many modern men are discovering these ancient practices in an effort to deepen their sexuality and discover their relationship with spirituality. Dolores La Chappelle's book, *Sacred Land, Sacred Sex, Rapture of the Deep* explores this theme in depth, connecting sexuality with sensitivity toward Nature.

Holding the spiritual view of sexuality, we can manifest the positive vibrations of Ares/Mars—the energy, assertiveness, and power. As Thomas Moore writes, "The soul, tradition has taught us for centuries, needs the profound and challenging grace of Mars, who reddens everything in his vicinity with the glow of passionate life, brings a creative edge to every action, and sows the seeds of power in every moment and event. When Mars is overlooked and undervalued he is forced to appear in fetish and in violent behavior. Mars is infinitely greater than personal expression of anger. Creative and destructive, he is life itself poised for struggle."[11]

RELATIONSHIP WITH FATHER

Poor Ares never had a loving father or mentor to guide him. Zeus rejected him and strongly favored his other sons, Hermes and Apollo. As the all powerful Sky God and King, Zeus operated in the mode of "power over" or authority from above (commonly called patriarchy). Not knowing how to empower his sons or share wisdom, he could only provide a bad example. Ares spent his life battling and bedding many adversaries, not unlike his father.

We read of so many men whose fathers were abusive or alcoholic. Having no other role models, they too assumed these patterns. In many cases, fathers lead such empty mechanized lives during the day that it is difficult for them to feel their sense of power or self-worth.

RITUALS FOR WORKING WITH ARES ENERGY

RAGE

For these rituals, it is important to have a fire, preferably a bonfire outdoors, though an indoor fireplace will do. Fire symbolizes heat and anger and purifies those who wish to clear the emotions. A large space provides room to move. Next to the fire set up an altar using objects representing the four directions and photographs of ancestors or modern men who personify true warriors. Men should bring large drums and other instruments to accompany their movements.

To begin, smudge the area. While the men are drumming, a smudge bowl is passed around with cedar, sage, or other purifying incense. Each man smudges the person next to him. The drumming continues, builds to a peak, and stops.

The leader or four different men call in the directions:

> To the East, we call in the golden eagle, the spirit of the warrior, who flies over all.

> To the South, we call in fire and deep passion, the warmth we feel in our hearts, our brother the coyote who fills us with his humor.

> To the West, we call in the forces of dusk and night, our friend the owl who provides us with inner sight.

> To the North, we call in the ancient buffalo, who brings us wisdom from the ancestors.

As the talking stick is passed, each man shares the source of his rage and those times in his life where he has experienced anger.

In the second part of the ritual, the lights or candles are put out and only the light of the fire is present. One or two men should take charge of the fire so that they can tend it while the movement is taking place. The men place their drums and instruments in the center of the circle. They then begin to move, chant, scream, or whatever else comes through to express their rage. At any point, one can choose a drum or other instrument to play so that a whole scenario emerges with each man focused on his inner expression. After the energy feels complete, one man lights some candles (or a small lamp if indoors) and all return to their places in the circle.

For a few minutes there should be quiet, allowing each to center and recapitulate his experience in his own mind. Whoever feels motivated may then take the talking stick and share any insights he has gained from the ritual. These sharings should be brief and from the heart; too much analyzing and mental energy at this point will destroy the effect of the ritual. It is a good idea for all to go home and to share furthur at a future time. The ritual can end with a few chants and the holding of hands around the circle.

RITUAL FOR SEXUALITY

At another time, a group of men may choose to focus their ritual on sexuality and sensuality. What is balanced sexuality and how can one practice sacred sex? Regardless of whether they are heterosexual, homosexual, or bi–sexual, the men can share what their needs are sexually with a partner, and how they have incorporated other practices such as tantra to enjoy a more complete sexual experience.

After sharing, the men stand up and move around as if making love to all of nature—the earth, sky, trees, plants. Some may wish to play instruments or drum while others move and dance. As each becomes aware of the depths of his sexual nature and how it encompasses all beings, he may wish to move with others or with several others, flowing with the natural rhythms, looking into their eyes, and feeling the energy move in their hearts.

When the energy is complete, songs and chants may be shared that focus on love and opening up the heart.

MENS EXPERIENCES

BARTON STONE

As a child, my fascination with war made me draw complex battle scenes of World War II fighter planes and navy ships, falling bombs and shells and puffy explosions until the whole sheet was a smudge of graphite. In these drawings no prisoners were taken.

Later, in adolescence, this warrior urge was seen in my "tough guy" stance and the righteous belligerence that young men unsure of themselves often display. I both feared and thrilled to the adrenalin rush of physical confrontation with other boys, in or out of the sports arena.

Such behavior on a collective scale in the nuclear age was clearly suicidal and intolerable. Influenced by Buddhism, Hinduism, and Gandhi, I wanted to live without harming others and to be a pacifist. My Ares nature still came out, however, transforming my philosophical pacifism into active resistance to nuclear war.

Gandhi's dilemma has always been with me—how to change a system based on power, force and violence without employing the very qualities I seek to change? How to be strong though unarmed? How to speak truth to confront power?

Living that dilemma, I began to see the healing warrior qualities of respect for boundaries, integrity of word and deed, and willing-ness to take responsibility. To be fully present in any situation, with full intention and mindfulness, is for me the manifestation of leadership and power.

RICK RAMIREZ

Ares energy to me is spontaneous gusto; it's going for what you want. It's the most repressed part of me because I try to figure things out ahead of time, to control the experience through my mind rather than use my physical force. Meditation practices have helped me to let go of control and deal with this part of my shadow. On the other hand, things do come out of my mouth in a blunt manner and later I'm sorry I've said them.

This has been a constant struggle for me—the unconscious Ares bursting out. Astrologically, I have Mars (Ares) in the sign Libra in the twelfth house which represents the unconscious or the more spiritual realm. Years ago, an astrologer told me that Groucho Marx had the same position of Mars. That helps me to understand why I have not always been out there in a physical way.

The true warrior represents the integration of the shadow; for me that means letting go of my control. It means trusting my intuition to know the appropriate timing and then to act immediately.

ENDNOTES

[1] Keen, Sam, *Fire in the Belly*, p.95.

[2] Moore, Robert, & Gillette, Douglas, *King, Warrior, Magician, Lover*, p.92.

[3] Moore, Thomas, *Care of the Soul*, p.127.

[4] *Larousse Encyclopedia of Mythology*, p.137.

[5] Graves, *The Greek Myths*, vol.1., p.73.

[6] Ibid., p.67.

[7] Ibid., p.68.

[8] Ibid., p.67.

[9] Bolen, Jean Shinoda, M.D., *Gods in Everyman*, p.195.

[10] Ibid., p.199.

[11] Moore, Thomas, p.129.

Invocation to ZEUS

High on Mt. Olympus,

Zeus, with your thunderbolt,

and scepter,

Ruling over

Gods and mortals,

Lusting after women,

Creating a new race,

Fathering,

Guiding.

Zeus

Chapter 6

THE FATHER GOD COMPLEX—
THE MYTH OF ZEUS

he father, whether a personal father or our father in heaven, has ruled the realm since the Sky God Zeus led the other Olympian gods and goddesses. The father's role is an authoritarian one for he sets down the laws and structure of society. As king, his personal destiny reflects the destiny of the country he rules. If the king prospers and is well, so does his realm. If the king is ill or incapacitated, drought, famine, poverty and wars may follow. The personal father controls the mother and the children much as the king controls his subjects. Whether he goes out to hunt game or puts on a business suit each morning, he is supposed to provide a home for the family and food. To his family, father is God and his power is strong. But when the father does not perform his role, is abusive or absent, the family unit falls apart. When responsibility is given to the eldest son or falls on other sons, resentment often occurs. The dynamic between the irresponsible father and overly responsible son may take generations to resolve.

Many pre-patriarchal agricultural societies focused their rituals on a king to ensure the fertility of the land and the well being of the people. The king as priest acted as an intercessor between humans and gods; he was regarded as a god himself, able to bring rain and sun and harvests. Many such societies believed that if a king were old, frail or dead, his kingdom, too, would wither and die. Consequently, people sought to keep the spirit of the king alive by transfering his soul, which represented his power, to a younger more vital being before old age and weakness set in. Rituals were established whereby the old king was slain and the new king imbued with his powers.

Pre–patriarchal societies also revered a queen. Their sacred marriage took place on May day or on other pagan festivals. They were originally known as the king and queen of the wood.[1] In the Eleusinian mysteries, the union of the Sky God Zeus with the Corn Goddess Demeter was represented by the union of the hierophant with a priestess of Demeter. An ear of corn symbolized the fertilization of the Sky God by the Corn Goddess.[2] Though vital to these early societies, the king was not the sole authority figure, but one half of a team or partnership.

In later times, however, the function of fertility was perceived as masculine and there was not a balance in the relationship between king and queen. Father gods like Zeus or the Egyptian Amun-Ra pursued sexual relationships with goddesses and mortal women; they were always portrayed as dominant. Woman's role diminished to that of a sexual plaything or babymaking incubator.

SHADOW SIDE OF THE FATHER GOD

The shadow side of the father/god/king is the authoritarian or tyrant. The tyrant theme has been played out on a grand scale in history by Hitler and Mussolini, more recently by Saddam Hussein. On a smaller scale, it is played out daily by the father who beats his children, the husband who abuses his wife, the boss who harasses his secretary. Such men have taken on the role of God or King and consider themselves the ultimate authorities. But underneath their hard, often abusive, shells lie massive insecurities.

Throughout the ages, various religions have become tyrannical in their attempts to impose their version of the truth on humankind. Perhaps the most intense example of this was the Roman Catholic Church which killed, burned and tortured millions during the Inquistion. Countries and ethnic groups have also played the role of the tyrannical despot. Witness the recent war in Boznia-Herzogovina where the Serbs, perceiving themselves as superior, have not only sought to dominate Croats and Muslims by taking over the land, but by raping and impregnating women.

MYTH OF ZEUS

Zeus, the most powerful god on Mt. Olympus, wielded the thunderbolt, controlled the motion of the heavenly bodies, pronounced oracles, passed laws and punished transgressors, gave power and authority to kings and was revered as the "father of the Gods". He was not, in fact, their father though he earned the role of father figure. Thanks to his mother, Rhea, young Zeus escaped the fate of his sisters and brothers who were eaten by their Titan father Cronus. Having earlier gupled down Poseidon, Hades, Hestia, Demeter and Hera, (and apparently bored with the sport), Cronus failed to note that a stone wearing swaddling clothes was standing in for baby Zeus. Zeus was taken to a cave in Crete where he was brought up by nymphs. After he grew to manhood, Zeus visited his mother who mixed Cronus a magic potion which caused him to vomit up the children he had eaten years before. With his newly revived brothers, Zeus then waged a war against the Titans, who chose Atlas as their leader because Cronus was too old.[3]

Zeus married repeatedly and impregnated many women, both

mortal and immortal. With his first wife, the Titaness Metis, he fathered the goddess of war Athena. With his second wife Themis, daughter of Uranus and Gaia, he fathered the Seasons and the Fates. Yet another wife was the Titaness Mnemosyne who gave birth to nine daughters, the Muses.[4] Eventually he married Hera who gave birth to Ares, Hephaestus and Hebe. The match was not made in heaven. Zeus and Hera bickered constantly for Zeus did not trust his wife. Hera, for her part, constantly tried to humiliate and trick Zeus, and on occasion borrowed Aphrodite's girdle to stir his passion and weaken his will.[5]

In time, Zeus' overweening pride led all the Olympians except Hestia to bind him with rawhide thongs, tied with a hundred knots. Thetis the Nereid, foreseeing a civil war on Olympus, brought in the hundred handed Briareus, who untied the thongs, using every hand at once. Free again, Zeus punished Hera by hanging her from the sky with golden bracelets around her wrists and anvils weighting her ankles until her cohorts swore never to rebel again.[6]

Zeus' philandering went far beyond Olympus. He was the swan who seduced Leda, the white bull who carried off Europa and the sun that sent the shower of gold that impregnated Danae. When Demeter spurned his advances, Zeus changed himself into a bull, raped her and impregnated her with Persephone.[7]

Zeus was also attracted to men. The Trojan youth Ganymede, kidnapped by Zeus'eagle, served as Zeus' cupbearer and probably love slave as well. Hermes, the boy's father, received a pair of fine white horses in compensation. Ganymede has been immortalized in the constellation Aquarius the water bearer.[8]

As a father, Zeus was sometimes protective, other times destructive. He saved the aborted fetus of his son Dionysus by carrying him in his own thigh until Dionysus was ready to be born. Proud of his daughter Athena, who was born fully armed from his head, Zeus gave her power objects and fulfilled her every wish. He rejected his son Ares and threw Hephaestus off Olympus, permanently injuring his foot. Worst of all, he permitted Hades to abduct Persephone.

Although Zeus' frequent sperm donations are generally seen in the light of idle "macho" conquest, he aimed to be the progenitor of a new race. Having killed off the Titans, Zeus created the race of Oympians in his own image.

THE SHADOW SIDE AS SEEN IN THE ZEUS MYTH

SEXUAL AFFAIRS AND DECEPTION

Zeus certainly represents the philanderer who is ready to assume any role or in Zeus' case, any form to make a conquest. This part of the male takes greater pleasure in scoring than in the actual act of love-making. Emotionally distant, the Zeus type considers sex to be a sport or pursues relationships that are useful socially or politically.

When these sexual liaisons involve deception and dishonesty, jilted wives may take the tack of Hera and respond vindictively.

Like Zeus, the average western man sees woman as some dark forbidden territory that he must conquer. He resents the fact that she is able to stir his desire nature and that he cannot exist without her. His defense is to treat her as an object of conquest which is of no benefit to anyone.

As Sam Keen explains, "If I am suspicious, or angry, or self-absorbed, I will come to her with a tight, defended body. I will be unable to allow the slow, soft pulsations, the ascending involuntary rhythms of deepening pleasure. Our movements will have the quality of a battle. I will try to make her respond so that I may prove myself superior to her. If I approach her merely as a body, a piece, an instrument designed to give me pleasure I also reduce my body to a machine divorced from feeling, a set of nerve endings that may be stimulated to produce pleasurable, or painful sensations"[9]

John Stoltenberg adds, "Sexual freedom has never really meant that individuals should have sexual self-determination, that individuals should be free to experience the integrity of their own bodies and be free to act out of that integrity in a way that is totally within their own right to choose. ....Sexual freedom has never really been about **sexual justice between men and women.** It has been about maintaining men's superior status, men's power over women; and it has been about sexualizing women's inferior status, men's subordination of women."[10]

AUTHORITY/FATHER FIGURE

Zeus was a father/authority figure who inspired fear in other Olympians and respect tinged with fear in his children. If anyone got out of line, he hurled the thunderbolt and everything went up in flames. To this day, the expression "lightening strikes" refers to the fiery and unexpected power of a Zeus figure.

Most of today's father/kings order and punish their subjects abusively because of their own fears and frustrations. Discipline is possible, however, from a place of understanding, compassion and enlightenment. In his book, *The Prince and the King*, Michael Gurian refers to the "sacred wound" given by the Sacred King to his son. A sacred wound builds the son's own strength, self-assertiveness and confidence. It must come from a place of love, intimacy and respect between father and son and not from abuse.

Boys constantly seek some proof of their manhood; those who prove themselves by sexual exploits or gang initiations demonstrate their bravery and strength at the expense of a victim or victims. By asserting their **power over** someone, they harm others as well as neglect the development of their own caring nurturing sides. For a boy to blossom into manhood he must undergo an initiation that develops his inner strength and enables him to trust himself in a deeper way. Native American vision quests test the flexibility and inner strength of boys and force them to confront feelings of being scared, alone and vulnerable. Afterwards, the boy knows his own strength and power. Having made a spiritual connection, he can call on this power in times of adversity.

Unfortunately, most boys these days do not have a positive father figure to initiate them into manhood. Many have struggled under tyrannical fathers who constantly wield their thunderbolts. In turn, these boys grow up to abuse their own sons. Rage rather than healthy anger is the dominant emotion displayed.

Sons of authoritarian fathers grow up thinking they must be perfect in every way. This perfectionism robs them of the ability to **feel,** to experience their emotions and set their own standards.

Unlike the sacred king, the modern father usually feels frustrated and diminished in his work; the mechanization, emptiness and isolationism he experiences fail to feed his spiritual being or provide him with a sense of his own self-worth. It becomes difficult to transfer any sense of inner power and self-esteem to a son. At home, where the father is in the mother's teritory, he may feel more alienated from his children. Some fathers attempt to gain affection by taking on the role of the indulgent father or to gain sympathy by drinking and other addictive behavior. Men with even less self-esteem take out their frustrations through violent and abusive behavior and know of no way to establish an emotional connection with their families.

The son who sees his father in a weak and vulnerable state feels disillusioned and abandoned by the one person who was his role model. He no longer has a sense of his father but sees only the shadow of the man. In order to keep on with his life, a son must **repress** his emotions and let his own dreams and ideals wither. If his father is authoritarian and verbally abusive, he must also repress the sense of his own power. If his father is violent and physically abusive, he will escape, however he can.

Even at his best, the Sky Father Zeus was an inadequate ineffective parent. Good fathers need to become Earth Fathers, which is nurturing as well as protective. A modern Earth Father can switch roles with the mother; he can remain at home while the mother goes out; he can help with household chores, with homework, with the dressing of young children, with the telling of myth and reading of bed-time stories. In this way, a more balanced role exists between mother and father. Sons, then, have a role model with which to find the nurturing qualities in themselves and they do not have to shift their allegiance from mother to father at a certain age. A mother married to an Earth Father can assume some of the sky functions giving her son reason to regard her as a heroine and protector.

ZEUS AS MOTHER

Zeus carried Dionysus in his thigh until he was ready to be born; Athena also was born from the head of Zeus. In fact, the Zeus archetype does carry out some of the female functions. Men taking over feminine roles is prevalent in our society, especially in the male doctors who presume to understand the feminine body and are in charge of delivering babies. Scientific knowledge and emotional distance replaces intuitive knowledge and emotional closeness. It is much healthier, both physically and emotionally, to have a new born baby taken by the hands of a midwife or grandmother than by a doctor's forceps. (In fact, much cranial damage is done at birth by the forceps.)

In the 1990's we have another way in which men are taking over feminine roles. This is in the arena of in vitro fertilization and growing sperm in test tubes. Modern science, once again, has taken the reproductive function away from the mother and placed it in the laboratory. As always, there is a choice here—whether mother and father wish to become Earth Mother and Earth Father for their children, or whether they give over the reins of control to the scientists.

RITUALS FOR WORKING WITH THE ZEUS FATHER ARCHETYPE

This ritual is one of the most important in this book, as every man has issues to work out with his own father or those men who have been father figures for him.

Prior to participating in this ritual, each man should think about and write something based on several questions. How do I feel about my own sense of power? How do I act in relationships? What was my relationship with my father like? Was my father an honest man, was he loving, did he have a sense of his own power, did he enjoy and love life? In what ways do I resemble my father? What other men were important for me in my life? What traits did they have that I desire to emulate? Who were my early heroes in literature, mythology, films?

After the place used for the ritual is smudged, the men set up an altar with photographs of elders, wise men and personal fathers in addition to objects symbolizing the four directions. Personal power objects should also be placed on the altar.

Drumming and rattling begin while the men smudge each other.

The man or High Priest leading the ritual or several men call in directions.

> To the East, we invoke the spirit of the golden
> eagle and the God Zeus,

To the South, we call in fire, warmth, and passions and we invoke the God Brahma from India, (Brahma along with Vishnu and Siva represent the divine father in India.)

To the West, we call in the depths and the darkness, the ancient God, Ahura-Mazda, (Ahura Mazda is the Zorastrian father-god.)

To the North, we invoke the wisdom of the elders and the God of the Norse, Odin. (Odin is the Norse father authority figure).

Each man in the circle shares what he has written or thought about in preparation for this ritual. He also shares how he has been helped by his father and what he needs to heal.

In the second part of the ritual, one man leads a journey to the grandfather circle. This is a circle of elders who exist in the spirit world. Each man closes his eyes, breathes deeply and focuses on the drumbeat as he goes down into the lower realm and meets the grandfathers. Once there, he asks the grandfathers what he needs to know at this time regarding his own development and power and what it is he needs to heal with his father.

After journeying, a grandfather dance begins. Each man first dances with his own father, working out the love, hate, fear and other emotions he has experienced. Then he dances with his grandfather or one of his other relatives. Last, he dances with one of the ancient grandfathers or elders, allowing his spirit to come through and nurture him.

When the dance is complete, all share their experiences and may plan other rituals where individual men can work out feelings with their fathers, speak with their fathers and forgive them in the supportive environment of the group.

The ritual ends with chanting, holding hands in the circle and thanking the gods who were invoked earlier.

MEN'S EXPERIENCES

BARTON STONE

However powerful my mother seemed to me as an infant, I was quite aware that my father superseded her with his power; my mother and I were always subject to his moods and desires. I believe this was communicated before I understood speech; my mother's body would subtly tense when he came into our presence. Our games would stop or become subdued as though our good times were offensive to him.

My father was a Christian minister, doing his best for the rural southern congregations that he served. He wrote hymns and devotional poetry. In eloquent sermons he described a God who loved humans so much that he sacrificed his only son, the reasoning of which escaped me. In his life, my father modeled an image of a god who was paternalistic, judgmental and emotionally preoccupied.

As soon as I was old enough to leave his home, I did, as well as leaving his church. I had had quite enough of a God who was like my father.

Later I was attracted to Zen Buddhism, which avoided beliefs about God and concentrated on the practice of sitting in meditation. My images were my own, but I found quickly that the Buddhist community was another benevolent patriarchy with the abbot assuming the role of Father/God.

As my political consciousness grew during the decades of the nuclear arms race, world leaders posed like frightened adolescents, insanely willing to poison and destroy the earth to prove their manhood.

The earth! Her hills and canyons, her meadows and streams restored a sense of deity to me that has no need for concepts such as king, lord, or sovereign. Much as we humans may feel compelled to balance dualities, Mother Earth seems to do quite well with an original female primacy that sometimes produces sons for reasons of her own.

Our manhood! We men have such talents for beauty, entertainment and elaboration, but our five thousand year experience of usurping authority over society has been disastrous. May our future kingly pursuits be to clean up the messes we have made, to play on the floor with children and to praise the divine attributes of the Mother.

RICK RAMIREZ

I've never related to Zeus as a wise being but mostly as a strong leader; to me the most fascinating part about him is that he threw thunderbolts. Growing up in the Vietnam era, I've always been aware of what Robert Bly calls the betrayal of the son. There were no protective fathers around then. As a male archetype, Zeus has had his day and we need to supplant him with newer more earth centered gods.

My own father was very authoritative and had the power that comes from that mode of being. There was no question about my obeying him, although he did listen to my ideas as well. I feel he let me have a long leash. He was also a good care taker and provider; he started saving for college when each of his children was born. At fourteen, when my parents divorced, I was separated from him. We came back together in my twenties when I helped him get his first books published as part of the spreading of the Puerto Rican culture. Our relationship then became one of partnership and friendship.

I feel he gave me a lot of challenges when I was growing up and

I'm thankful for them. He sent me to a Wilderness Survival camp in Wyoming when I was thirteen; I was a very scared city boy but I survived, though not unscathed. I know that he respected me because none of my other siblings were given this challenge.

ENDNOTES

[1] see Sir James Frazer, *The Golden Bough*.

[2] Frazer, Sir James, *The Golden Bough*, p.165.

[3] Graves, Robert, *The Greek Myths*, vol.1., pp.39–40.

[4] *Larousse Encyclopedia of Mythology*, pp.105–106.

[5] Graves, vol.1., p.53

[6] Ibid., p.54.

[7] *Larousse Encyclopedia of Mythology*, pp.110–111.

[8] Bolen, Jean Shinoda, M.D., *Gods in Everyman*, p.49.

[9] Keen, Sam, *The Passionate Life*, pp.167–168.

[10] Stoltenberg, John, *Refusing To Be a Man*, p.127.

Invocation to HADES

Oh Hades,

Lord of the underworld,

Deep down in the earth,

Dancing with Persephone,

Guiding souls who enter,

Helping them with darkness

and chaos,

fear and transformation.

Hades, dark god of the realm below.

Hades

Chapter 7

RAPE, DEATH, AND THE UNDERWORLD—
THE MYTH OF HADES

The god Hades has long inspired fear in humans as might be expected of a god whose very name was given to the underworld. Hades represents the darkest side of man's shadow. He is the other half of the Sky God, Zeus. Together, they are like Inanna and Ereshkigal of Sumerian legend, or the modern Dr. Jekyll and Mr. Hyde.

The man who is in touch with Hades explores his deepest fears. Most often, this happens as a result of some major life crisis—the death of a loved one, ending of a relationship, loss of a job, or the destruction of a home. Like Achilles and other Greek heroes, he finds himself forced unexpectedly into the realm of Hades. However, a man **can also** choose to visit Hades willingly. To confront his own soul, he may go on a vision quest, a meditation retreat or a pilgrimage. He can also pursue psychological or spiritual therapies where the probing of unconscious material will uncover repressed events of his past.

Being in prison is another way to enter Hades, an enforced

isolation where one grapples with his own truth. From prison came the writings of Malcolm X and the insights of Nelson Mandela. Imprisonment is the physical reality of the psychological state that most men fear.

The Greek underworld symbolizes the unconscious, the dark, the lower depths and fear itself. For centuries now, Hades has been analogous to the Christian's concept of Hell, so well described by Dante in the Inferno. Because patriarchal Christians refuse to explore the dark and prefer to see it only as the realm of sin, Hades became the domain of Satan and evil forces. In contrast, Norse mythology holds that "hell" is a uterine shrine or sacred cave of re–birth.[1] Hel was the name of the Norse queen of the underworld. This concept of "hell" as a cauldron or womb may also be found in the Pacific where Pele, the Hawaiian volcano goddess, bears striking similarities to the goddess Hel.

MYTH OF HADES

Hades was one of the sons of Cronus and Rhea who was swallowed by his father. After he was regurgitated, Hades joined Zeus and Poseidon against Cronus and defeated the Titans. When the brothers drew lots for portions of the world, Hades received the underworld. The best known myth about Hades is the abduction of Persephone. Persephone was playing in the meadows with her friends when she was drawn to a beautiful narcissus. As she was admiring the narcissus, the earth opened up and Hades appeared with his chariot. Hades grabbed Persephone while she screamed for her father Zeus who ignored her cries since he had already approved Hades' violent scheme. As the earth closed up, Hades' horses brought Persephone to the underworld.

Demeter, Persephone's mother, mourned with such anguish that all plant life on earth withered and died. When famine was inevitable, Zeus sent Hermes to fetch Persephone from the underworld. Before she stepped into Hermes' chariot, Hades gave Persephone some pomegranate seeds to eat. Because she ate six seeds, she was forced to return to the underworld for six months each year to reign as Hades' queen.

The myth of Hades and Persephone, in fact, is related to the Eleusinian Mysteries. The Eleusinian Mysteries were ceremonies of the goddess Demeter which were enacted yearly; initiates learned to access inner states by going down into the underworld and consequently no longer feared death.

RELATIONSHIP OF HADES MYTH TO THE MALE SHADOW

Rape

Hades captured Persephone by force and without her consent, a way that men relate to women that they desire or wish to have power over. This myth portrays woman as an object to be conquered.

In his essay "Sexual Objectification and Male Supremacy", John Stoltenberg points out that women are no longer subjects and equal when they are perceived as **objects** for sexual gratification. When men relate to women as objects, they become completely oblivious to their feelings and what happens to them. Total objectification makes possible gang rape and the mass rapes committed during war. Turning women into objects has also given rise to pornography where the female body is exploited as a sexual stimulant. This dehumanization of women eventually leads to sexual violence and rape.

Although women bear the children, somehow these children become the property of the men. A child that is not "owned" by a man is considered "illegitimate" or a "bastard" when, in fact, he/she has been birthed solely by the mother. This is a law established by the patriarchy in early times which still holds weight today. The mother, who carries the child for nine months and births the child, is robbed of her power and placed in the position of a slave.

Men often rape their wives, considering it their right and her a piece of their property. Lorena Bobbitt, who cut off her husband's penis, was in all probability a long term victim of abuse and rape. In his book, *Earth Honoring—The New Male Sexuality*, Robert Lawlor discusses the patriarchal image of the Sky Father whose active aggressive sperm impregnates passive women and reduces the sexual act to one of procreation. Earlier earth–based religions had believed that it was possible for a woman to become pregnant without the help of physical sperm. Austrailian aborigines think that procreation occurs in two ways—one called Sperm Children and the other called Spirit Children. Spirit energy, related to deceased ancestors, often accumulates in the earth in rocks and trees and could enter into a woman's body.[2] This mystical view of parthogenesis was an aspect of the Dionysian fertility cults, later absorbed into Roman Christianity as the idea of the Virgin Birth.[3] According to some accounts, Dionysus, like Christ, was conceived with divine inspiration through Zeus' spiritual impregnation of Semele.

Once the understanding of conception shifted to a biological function, the concept of death also changed. In the old religions, spirit went back to earthy and natural forms; patriarchal religion replaced this with a spiritual ascent to heaven. One of the old symbols for procreation in earth–based religions was a serpent dripping fluid from its tail into a cup–like vessel. As the patriarchy developed, the symbol became a penis spurting semen, replacing the idea of the fecundating power of the Earth herself.[4]

With Hades/Pluto energy dominant, feminine sexuality became intensely repressed. Women could not display their innate sensuality because it was mis–interpreted as a "come–on" to men.

Women were not supposed to have any sexual pleasure and were not to indulge in sex except to create a child.

Centuries of this attitude are still apparent in the way women dress and act. There are still many places in the Western world where women can not nurse a baby in public. Women must constantly hide their breasts; those who expose or accentuate them in any way are often branded as whores or prostitutes. In many countries of Africa, women are still being given sexual initiations that are painful and unsafe, where the clitoris, the organ of sexual stimulation, is removed. Sex becomes a painful preamble to the biological function of child bearing, which is also very painful and hazardous after these "surgeries."

Fathers who rape their daughters and men who look the other way also subscribe to the Hades/Persephone myth. Like Hades, they rape and keep their action under cover. Like Zeus (who was also a rapist), they ignore the cries. Whether the father is intoxicated and chooses not to remember it afterward, or he feels it is his right because he is the patriarch of the family, the daughter's violation remains unacknowledged. Unfortunately, many mothers are so fearful of losing their own position in the household that they do not rally to their daughters' aid. This causes more trauma to the daughter who often ends up repressing the whole affair, only to deal with it years later in therapy.

DEATH

Fear of dying is great among most people because death implies a loss of power and control; we do not know what the next stage is. Without a spiritual belief that connects death to the process of life, the fear becomes intense.

Death has always been associated with dark events—a life threatening illness, a kidnapping, a murder, an accident. It is rarely thought of as a gradual process of disintegration, of the body's wearing out and going back to the earth.

In contrast, many native cultures encourage people to start preparing for death at mid–life, around forty. Each day then becomes a time to let go of something or to clear up relations with others so that one is free to leave life with a clear conscience.

TRANSFORMATION

Hades appears when a life crisis is imminent. A man then has no choice but to make the pilgrimage into his own lower depths where he might uncover memories of illness, hurt, emotional betrayal and depression. He also might remember the loss of someone he loved when he was young.

Fears, long since buried, surface when one enters the realm of Hades. Confronting these fears and working with them can lead to transformation. Keeping them buried creates even more stress because the personality uses up vast amounts of energy playing a role and holding down the repressed material. As one gets older, this becomes more and more difficult and often leads to major physical symptoms, life threatening illness and emotional breakdowns. Quite literally, the stuff under the rug begins to decompose and smell!

The midlife crisis often corresponds to the astrological cycle of the planet Pluto(Hades) which "squares" (a 90 degree angle) Pluto in one's natal birth chart around the age of 45. (Recently some have been getting this "transit" as early as 38 or 39 because the orbit of Pluto has moved inside Neptune's orbit, thus being closer to earth.) During this time, we are often faced with major life changes. Moving to another area of the country, leaving or being fired from one's job, breaking up a relationship are common. Sometimes the death of a loved one catalyzes inner growth; sometimes there is a serious accident or the diagnosis of a life threatening disease as lupus, cancer or AIDS. The message is always the same—**descend** into the underground for a close look at old patterns and fears. Those who face these fears and make changes in their lives, feel re-born. Emerging from the darkness is like emerging from the womb, with less baggage and more freedom.

According to Mark Gerzon, author of *Coming into Our Own: Understanding the Adult Metamorphosis,* "Men enter midlife in a landscape barren of useful landmarks, without traditions or stories to guide us over this unfamiliar terrain. We find our well-crafted life scripts suddenly running out. Money and titles and testosterone just don't do it for us anymore."[5] Reflecting on the midlife crisis, singer Kenny Loggins says, "Instead of a crisis, I refer to it as 'midlife clarity', because it can be a time of spiritual awakening if the individual is willing to look at and deal with everything that comes up in his life as honestly as possible. In my midlife clarity, it became easier for me to think and feel what was and wasn't working, and I simply kept the things that were."[6]

In the first half of life, men are busy building careers, competing with other men, controlling or ignoring nature and her cycles, and often dominating women. Around 40 there is a switch as men become more passive, more introspective, more in touch with nature and more compassionate toward women. Their projects may now involve personal therapy, spiritual awareness classes, hiking and camping and meditation. Women, on the other hand, often become more active in their careers and in the social and political realms.

Many men lose their jobs at midlife. In addition to confronting their own loss, there is the fear of providing for their families and making use of unscheduled time. This forces them to look deeply into their old patterns. A relative who lost his job in his mid-forties confided to me that he was forced to realize that life was more than just working at a job. Similarly, Richard Bolles, author of *What Color is Your Parachute?*, lost his tenure as canon pastor at Grace Cathedral church in San Francisco at the age of 43. His subsequent journey into the necessity of a career change resulted in his writing a book on the topic. Men who have careers as athletes or dancers or even some actors know that their time is limited. They know that they will have to undergo a type of death when they end their career.

A few men elect to make major transformations without being catalyzed by unexpected life changes. They may undertake a spiritual pilgrimage, participate in a meditation retreat, go on a vision quest. Some men step into the darkness through therapy, confronting the demons of their own unconscious. Like the myth of the Sumerian goddess Inanna who chose to go underground to visit her sister Ereshkigal, they have chosen this time to explore their own "lower depths." I knew a man in his mid–forties who spent a week camping in a tent totally blindfolded; he had his wife deliver food once a day and the rest of the time he spent in prayer and meditation, shutting out all external stimuli. At the end of the week, he felt much more in touch with who he was and what he wanted from life.

The rewards of the midlife period include re–birth, integration of conscious and unconscious personalities, and a feeling of wholeness. Yet exploring the realm of Hades may become a lifetime endeavor; there are always more layers to uncover.

POWER AND RICHES

For a "plutocrat," wealth is the means to attain power and dominate others. Hades/Pluto kept many riches in the underworld just as the earth holds valuable minerals. In politics money creates strong lobbies and controls votes. Most men know how unethical this type of behavior is but continue to play the game of "power over". The real treasures to be mined from Hades are the ability to be introspective, to live a reclusive life when necessary and get in touch with one's self.

UNDERWORLD AND THE MAFIA

Hades/Pluto, god of the underworld, clearly rules the shady worlds of drug dealing, organized crime and prostitution. Men who enter these realms live in their shadow side, dodging the law and creating their own moral and ethical codes.

Teenagers have been called the "black sheep" of their families because of drugs, sexual promiscuity, crime and general rebelliousnes. If they are not helped to find their own individual gifts, they may turn to a life of underworld activities as a way of protesting the structure of a society that hasn't supported their needs. Often they enter the underworld to leave behind lives of poverty, abuse and dysfunctional family situations. Once they enter, it is difficult to leave without another person or group catalyzing their transformation.

Politics—a world with its underside of corruption, wheeling and dealing— attracts power hungry males who give the illusion of ruling with Olympian detachment while pulling their strings in the realm of Hades. Curiously, the relatively powerless people who form grass roots opposition have come to be known as the political underground. Many political groups have started as underground forces—the ANC (African National Congress), IRA (Irish Republican Army), PLO (Palestinian Liberation Organization) to name a few.

Forays into the underworld must be integrated with a return to the world above if the shadow is both to express itself and change society.

RITUALS FOR HADES

RITUAL DEALING WITH RAPE

The first ritual deals with rape. It involves discussion of the desire to rape as well as ways to better understand the feelings of women (and men) who have been raped and those who fear being raped. How can men support those women and stop the rape of both women and the earth?

These rituals should be done in a dark place such as the basement of someone's house, an outdoor cave, a Native American kiva. Lighting with candles is preferable and the entire area should be cleansed with cedar, sage, sweetgrass or incense from cedar, pine, or juniper.

On an altar located in the center of the room place animal skulls, a bowl of dirt, and pictures of Hades/Pluto, Osiris, Freyr and other gods of the underworld. To honor the four directions, place in the East the wing feathers of birds associated with dark and night such as owls or ravens; in the South, a black candle; in the West, water in a chalice or cup and replicas of snakes or a snake skin; in the North, obsidian or smoky quartz crystals.

When the men gather in circle and prepare to drum, one man acts as High Priest and speaks to several others about calling in the directions and the God. The energy is built up through drumming, rattling and other instruments, and when it is appropriate, the High Priest or leader stops the drumming and begins calling in the directions.

> *To the East, we call in the spirits who will help us to reach a new beginning as we deal with change and transformation,*
>
> *To the South, we call in our passions and desires that we may look at them,*

To the West we invoke grandfather Owl, that he may guide us to move within,

To the North, we call in the ancient ones, the Elders, for their wisdom in exploring the deep dark places.

And now we invoke the god Hades/Pluto, lord of the underworld, to be with us and guide us.

After calling in the directions, a staff or talking stick is passed and each man recounts the times he has felt the desire to rape a woman (or another man) and if he has raped, his experience. The second part of the ritual deals with sexual desire and ways it can be manifested other than genital sex. Men may share their wisdom regarding Tantric and Taoist practices.

In the third part, men take pledges to support women and the earth and stop rape. Each man makes a pledge while the others bear witness to it.

In the last part of the ritual, there is drumming, sharing of chants, poems and songs.

RITUAL FOR TRANSFORMATION

The altar is set up as before but each man may want to place on the altar some symbol or photograph symbolizing his own transformation. Before coming to the ritual, each one should spend some time thinking about what it is that he needs to let go of. Where in his life is he stuck and what things are no longer working for him?

After drumming and calling in the directions and the gods, one man at a time comes to the middle of the circle and shares that place in himself where he wishes to change. While the others drum, each man may dance out his feelings and prayers, sing a chant, read a poem or anything else that expresses his deepest wishes for transformation. All pray with him to help these changes manifest.

If this is an on–going group, one session may be devoted to each man. If it is a ritual being held only once, time should be apportioned so that each has a chance to share and receive the prayers and support of the group. There should be a follow up ritual to see what changes each has manifested after three or six months.

At the end, drum, chant, and celebrate with feasting and dancing.

MENS EXPERIENCES WITH HADES

BARTON STONE

I experienced my first intense descent to the underworld as a young man awakening to the intellect. I was a student at Florida State University. Knowledge was an illusion; culture was deceptive; civilization was cruelty. Did anything matter? What an existential crisis!

I had real fear and despair. Everything I touched turned to ashes. There were some rewards as well—the feeling of a mythic journey full of danger and opportunity as well as a new and exciting identification with some of my favorite writers and poets.

Finally I took a bold step. I resolved to sit in the armchair in my shared apartment unitl I either died or understood the meaning of my life. My housemates were away and the solitude was dramatic.

The first hours seemed endless. I practiced every meditation technique I knew. I dialogued with many images of God, demanding and challenging them to show me some reason to live. I had conversations with T.S.Eliot, William Blake, W. B. Yeats, Swami Vivekananda and Franz Kafka. After several hours I decided it would be all right to leave the chair to pee and drink water. Food was not even tempting.

The gradual process of day turning into night was beautiful to observe without electric lights. I just sat and watched the shadows grow. How had I missed this for so long?

Waking fantasy, dreams and sleep were no longer separate in those long hours of darkness. I experienced feelings of fear and dread which were often accompanied by contradictory feelings of relief and freedom. Every thought or feeling I tried to grasp shifted and changed until I felt like I was falling freely through space. There was no bottom or place to stand. Was this Sartre's nausea? Was it the Zen emptiness, in and behind and through all form? Why did I have such a feeling of power and exhilaration? Falling felt almost like flying.

The room slowly lightened with the dawn and I knew that each moment was my choice: to live or die, love or hate, accept or defy. I was an outlaw. No rules could bind me for I alone was responsible for myself and the results of my choices. I could choose life and beauty, not because they were more real, but because they were my immediate preference. For me, God was dead and I was on my own.

When I chose to eat breakfast, I walked into a very vital world. The following weeks brought visions of the collapse of Western civilization with its problems of greed, hate and delusion. There was the indomitable urge for life in the plant world with the desire to consume all human ambition.

The lessons of that journey to the underworld were affirmed and expanded in later encounters with despair and change at midlife as well as in changes in relationships and career.

It has remained a model for my own process of transformation and one I use in guiding others on similar journeys through vision quests. Always one encounters despair, the willingness to die, the magical fluidity of experience, and a rebirth into freedom. The darkness of the underworld thus becomes both an ally and a birthright, the soul's backdrop for all endeavors.

RICK RAMIREZ

I've always liked dark places; as a young boy I created a den in the hedges. Later I started exploring the sewers which lured me because of their mysterious and labyrinth qualities. The dark places in nature symbolize for me the real mystery of our being.

When I got involved in spiritual growth, I was searching for "endarkenment" rather than enlightenment. I feel that our culture suppresses the dark side, even "New Age" philosophies exclude it from their field of vision. Real tranformation happens when one experiences the darkness, whether that is depression or alienation or fear. Affirming the positive is not enough. In Buddhism, the three causes of suffering are craving or grasping, fear or aversion and unconsciousness. If we are unconscious of our own darkness or push it away out of fear, we are creating our suffering in a very direct way.

I have always been attracted to catalysts that force me to look into my own darkness. I was turned off by psychedelic drugs because I had not heard of people using them in a serious way. Later, I encountered the work of Ram Dass and saw how he used them ritually to probe his own unconscious.

Rape is a strong issue. I was intensely attacted to my sister when she was ten and I was fourteen. I molested her but didn't get very far because of her resistance and my shame. Twenty years later it came up in her therapy; I had blocked it out. We had a good deal of communication about it which provided a strong healing between us. I realized that I was on the edge of puberty and was being overwhelmed by sensations for which I had no outlet. I had not been taught how to handle this energy. If sexuality were not repressed in our society and we were educated about it, there would be fewer rapes.

As Robert Lawlor explains in his book, *Earth Honoring—The New Male Sexuality,* repressed sexuality accounts for much of the mass destruction we have witnessed in this century. If we could learn how to use our sexuality in more gentle ways, we could transform the urge to rape and destroy. One way is the drumming and music in tribal cultures. There are many ways of love making that are sensitive and nurturing.

ENDNOTES

[1] Walker, Barbara, *The Women's Encyclopedia of Myths and Secrets,* p.380.

[2] Lawlor, Robert, *Earth Honoring —The New Male Sexuality,* p.79. (as explained in Max Charlesworth et al *Religion in Aboriginal Australia,* pp.125-131).

[3] Lawlor, p.79.

[4] Ibid., p.80.

[5] "Men on Midlife," article in *New Age Journal,* Aug. 1993, p.53.

[6] "Men on Midlife," p.54

Chapter 8

CONCLUSION

any changes and transformations have occurred for men who have worked with their shadow side. They have connected with parts of their being that lay buried for years, experienced grief and pain along with joy and ecstasy. For us women, exploring our male shadow has cleaned out many old cobwebs and freed our energy.

When men and women work with the shadow together, the experience can be intensely transformative as a result of the deep sharings and communications. After a ritual involving Dionysus, one man revealed that homosexuality was deeply embedded in his shadow. He was married, enjoyed his marriage and women but also felt great love for men. After discussing this, he realized that it was okay to love other men, embrace them and dance with them without feeling guilty. To be fully human is to experience the gamut of deep emotions. Another man used the term "responsible ecstasy" to describe this experience. So much of what lurks in our individual shadow is what society has condemned as wrong; in this case, not fitting the role model of the "macho" male.

After a ritual for Ares and discussion of male power, a man present shared that it was easy for him to identify with the overt physical power associated with maleness. However, he knew that there was another kind of power if he could only get in touch with his feminine side. This scared him, however, because he believed the feminine lacked force and strength. Finally, he did some past life regressions which enabled him to access a couple of life times in which he had been a woman. Remembering himself as a young female shaman, he experienced a kind of power that was different—it had softer edges, was not so outward but had a very strong and grounded feeling. Since that experience, he has not been afraid of his female side and has continued to access this deep inner power within.

Working with Hephaestus opened up deep caverns of repressed creative energy for many men. One man had always loved to sing until he auditioned for the high school chorus and was told he didn't have a good voice. For years, he sang by himself until, in a ceremony with other men, he forced himself to sing alone in the circle. The moment had come to let that part of himself out of the shadow. Now he spends much of his time singing, drumming and conducting ceremonies.

Rituals involving Hades are rarely comfortable and often involve emotional pain as past memories flood consciousness. During one of these rituals, a man got in touch with himself as a five year old boy experiencing the death of his father. He shed many tears which he had formerly held back because his mother and other relatives had told him to be strong. As he cried, he also felt deep compassion for that young five year old who lost the love and security of his father.

While exploring the energies of the Horned God, one man felt the surfacing of a tremendous amount of anguish. He had grown up on a farm in the mid-west and as a young boy, had helped with the work. Plowing the fields, he often felt he was disturbing the nature beings that dwelt there. He buried this feeling many times, thinking it a childish fantasy out of keeping with adult responsibilities. Had he ever spoken to his parents about this, they would have made fun of him. So he continued to do what felt wrong to his inner being. Only after these many years, was he able to express his emotion and ask forgiveness of the Horned God.

Another deep sharing occurred after a ceremony with Zeus energy. This particular person had been a math teacher in a ghetto school, playing the role of the strict disciplinarian and exacting father. Though some of the kids obeyed him, many rebelled. During this time, he fell in love with a soft, gentle woman who was also a teacher but had a very different approach. She was quite successful in her role as a disciplinarian because she assumed a nurturing and loving attitude toward her students, while keeping strong boundaries. As he adapted her style to his own classes, more friendships developed between him and his students. There was less rebellion, more genuine affection and the students were more motivated to do their work.

During a ritual of opening up and clearing with one's mother (see chapter IV), someone shared the following: the ritual he attended was led by a female shaman. On the far side of the room was an altar; while drumming and chanting, this man experienced tremendous love coming from the center of the altar. Whenever he looked toward the altar, he felt unconditional love and bliss pouring out of him. After the drumming stopped, he asked permission of the shaman to go up to the altar and see what was in the center. As he got closer, he sensed the energy of a cosmic mother who never stopped sending love to her children; he could feel the tremendous compassion and sacrifice that she poured out all day long without stopping. Finally, when he approached the altar, he saw a picture of the Virgin of Guadalupe and her child. It was such a powerful experience that he began working with the Guadalupe in ritual and has been led furthur into experiencing other Black Madonnas.

As these stories show, feelings that have been unconscious for many years can burst forth and become integrated into conscious awareness and action. When the participants recognized and abandoned old patterns, they attained more energy and a deeper feeling of harmony with natural rhythms.

Working with the myths of the gods and goddesses can help us all to open up the shadow side and to deeply explore the unconscious. May we all encounter the yin and yang of our beings and walk in balance on the earth!

BIBLIOGRAPHY

Anderson, William. *Green Man—The Archetype of our Oneness with the Earth.* San Francisco, CA. Harper Collins, 1990.

Bly, Robert. *A Little Book on the Human Shadow.* San Francisco, CA. Harper & Row, 1989.
Iron John. New York, NY. Random House, 1990.

Bolen, Jean Shinoda M.D. *Gods in Everyman.* New York, NY. Harper & Row, 1989.

Colman, Arthur and Libby. *The Father—Mythology and Changing Roles.* Wilmette, IL. Chiron Publications, 1988.

Danielou, Alain. *Gods of Love and Ecstasy—The Traditions of Shiva and Dionysus.* Rochester, VT. Inner Traditions International, 1984.

Evans, Arthur. *The God of Ecstasy—Sex Roles and the Madness of Dionysus.* New York, NY. St. Martin's Press, 1988.

Farrar, Janet and Stewart. *The Witches God.* Custer, Washington. Phoenix Publishing Co., 1989.

Graves, Robert. *The Greek Myths, vol. 1 and 2.* Baltimore, MD. Penguin Publishing Co., 1955.

Gurian, Michael. *Mothers, Sons, and Lovers.* Boston, MA. Shambhala Publications, 1994.
The Prince and the King. Los Angeles, CA. Jeremy Tarcher/Perigee, 1993.

Harding, Christopher, Ed. *Wingspan—Inside the Men's Movement.* New York, NY. St. Martin's Press, 1992.

Johnson, Robert A. *Owning Your Own Shadow.* San Francisco, CA. Harper Collins, 1991.

Keen, Sam. *Fire in the Belly.* New York, NY. Bantam Books, 1991.
The Passionate Life. San Francisco, CA. Harper Collins, 1994.

Bibliography—contd.

La Chapelle, Dolores. *Sacred Land, Sacred Sex, Rapture of the Deep.* Silverton, CO. Finn Hill Arts, 1988.

Larousse Encyclopedia of Mythology. New York, NY. Prometheus Press, 1960.

Lawlor, Robert. *Earth Honoring—The New Male Sexuality.* Rochester, VT. Park Street Press, 1989.

Mazis, Glen. *The Trickster, Magician, & Grieving Man.* Santa Fe, NM. Bear & Co., 1994.

Moore, Robert & Gillette, Douglas. *King, Warrior, Magician, Lover.* San Francisco, CA. Harper Collins, 1990.

Moore, Thomas. *Care of the Soul.* New York, NY. Harper Collins, 1992.

Richardson, Alan. *Earth God Rising.* St. Paul, MN. Llewellyn Publications, 1990.

Rowan, John. *The Horned God.* London, England. Routledge & Kegan, 1987.

Starck, Marcia. *The Dark Goddess—Dancing With the Shadow.* Freedom, Ca. The Crossing Press, 1993.

Stewart, R. J. *Celtic Gods, Celtic Goddesses.* London, England. Blandford, 1990.

Stoltenberg, John. *Refusing To Be a Man.* New York, NY. Penguin Books, 1989.

The End of Manhood. New York, NY. Penguin Books, 1993.

Woodman, Marian. *The Pregnant Virgin.* Toronto, Canada. Inner City Books, 1988.

Zweig, Connie and Abrams, Jeremiah ed. *Meeting the Shadow.* Los Angeles, CA. Jeremy Tarcher, 1991.